THE 50-60 SOMETHING START-UP ENTREPRENEUR

Published by Experiential Pte Ltd. in Singapore.

Published simultaneously in the United States.

Publisher's Cataloging-in-Publication Data

Names: Wigglesworth, Pamela, 1958- .

Title: The 50-60 something start-up entrepreneur : how to quickly start and run a successful small business / Pamela Wigglesworth.

Description: Singapore : Experiential, 2019. | Summary: This book covers where and how to begin as an entrepreneur, walking the reader through product development, branding, pricing, distribution, and marketing to topics on the use of technology. It includes understanding the sales process and how to overcome overwhelm by outsourcing.

Identifiers: LCCN 2017916375 | ISBN 9781978159785 (pbk.) | ISBN 9789811150555 (ebook)

Subjects: LCSH: Entrepreneurship. | New business enterprises. | Older people – employment. | Small business. | BISAC: BUSINESS & ECONOMICS /New Business Enterprises. | BUSINESS & ECONOMICS / Small Business.

Classification: LCC HD62.7 W54 2019 (print) | LCC HD62.7 (ebook) | DDC 658 W54--dc23

LC record available at https://lccn.loc.gov/2017916375

Book cover design by Armend Meha

Edited by Louisa Bennion

Books are available at special discounts for bulk purchases for sales promotions or corporate use. For more inform contact books@experiential.sg

For general information about our other products, keynotes, and seminars please contact Experiential at courses@experiential.sg

THE 50-60 SOMETHING START-UP ENTREPRENEUR

HOW TO QUICKLY START AND RUN A SUCCESSFUL SMALL BUSINESS

PAMELA WIGGLESWORTH

Table of Contents

Table of Contents

Chapter 11
Suck It Up and Embrace Technology

Chapter 12
You MUST Become a Salesperson

Chapter 13
Overcoming Overwhelm

50–60 Something Start-up Entrepreneurs, or the New 50–60 Something Poverty Economy

There is no such thing as job security. It doesn't exist anymore. All over the world a quiet, increasingly forced exodus is happening within companies across multiple industries and demographics, yet one group is being affected in significant ways because their age puts them in a uniquely complex position.

This demographic has been in the workplace for at least 30 years. They are highly skilled and experienced professionals in their field and they have been in organizations for 10 or more years. They tend to be in senior positions and are paid comfortable salaries. The demographic I'm referring to is the 50- to 60-something employee.

The fact is workers in their 50s and 60s are leaving the corporate world, the military, and civil service, and they are leaving not necessarily by choice and often before they are financially able to retire and maintain their existing lifestyle. This is despite the value they bring to the table in terms of their experience, reliability and loyalty, mature judgement, and corporate knowledge.

Companies are downsizing and making employees redundant on a regular basis. For those in their 30s and 40s, finding a new job might not be a big issue. But losing your job in your 50s or 60s brings with it a host of major issues that can have both an immediate and long-term impact on your lifestyle, your family, and your financial well-being.

Out-of-work 50- to 60-somethings face issues that other age groups have yet to encounter, issues that will have a significant impact on their quality of life over the next 30 to 40 years.

The Perfect Storm on the Horizon

There is a storm looming on the horizon. It's not even on the radar, but it will significantly impact the livelihood and lifestyle of individuals in their 50s and 60s, particularly in first-world countries.

This perfect storm is the coming-together of five unique circumstances that, independently, are benign in nature; collectively their convergence is guaranteed to create a dramatic shift in how this group of individuals will live over the next three to five decades of their lives.

In the near future, men and women over 50 years of age will find themselves facing long-term unemployment or underemployment as they compete with companies partaking in the gig economy, which reduces or eliminates the need for full-time employees. Some may find themselves unexpectedly joining the Club Sandwich Generation, looking after four generations of family under one roof. Almost all of them can expect an extended lifespan of an additional 30 years, yet they must confront the realization that relying on a pension plan is not likely to meet their needs for living a full life well into their 80s or 90s.

This perfect storm will be dramatic and telling, with two unique outcomes in its aftermath: one group of individuals will barely survive in the new 50–60 Something Poverty Economy, while another will flourish and thrive as they drive the 50–60 Something Start-up Entrepreneur movement.

The storm is gathering for an entire generation, and most of them won't be prepared because in their world the sun is shining and there is not a cloud on the horizon.

Unemployment's Effects on People Over 50

Gone are the days of *Leave it to Beaver*, the 1950s US TV show, when one job was sufficient to support the entire family and where Ward Cleaver, the breadwinner husband, worked nine-to-five and was home for dinner, and could expect to work at the same company until he was ready to retire in his 60s.

Long-term employment doesn't exist anymore. Today it's rare that individuals stay with one company throughout their career, and most households require two incomes.

Despite a slowing job market recovery, employers in the US are creating new jobs every month. However, millions of older workers who want to find a job cannot find work. According to a review of government figures by the Schwartz Center for Economic Policy Analysis the jobless rate for workers over 55 was 12% in 2016.[1] In other words, 2.5 million older Americans want to be employed, yet they don't have a job.

In a survey conducted in 2013 by the American Association of Retired Persons (AARP), older workers were shown to need more time to look for work: 36 weeks, compared to 26 weeks for younger workers.[2] In the US, UK, and Australia, people over 50 years of age are more likely than any other demographic to be unemployed in the long term, and when older displaced workers do find new jobs, they typically go back to work for about 75% of their former pay.

According to the Center for Retired Research at Boston College, for 60% of older workers who experience job loss, this means involuntary early retirement. Individuals in the US who lose their steady income in the decade leading up to retirement will also see a reduction in future Social Security earnings, given the loss in credits used to calculate a worker's benefits. Moreover, filing for benefits a lot earlier than planned, as some older workers will be forced to do, can significantly affect lifetime benefits.

In the UK, where people aged 50 years and over represent a third of the population, the numbers of unemployed mature people are startlingly similar to those in the US. Of the 10.2 million Britons between 50 and the state pension age (currently 65 for men and this will gradually increase from 60 to 65 for women), 2.9 million (28%) are out of work. Of the 2.9 million, 1.7 million think it is unlikely that they will ever work again—an alarming number of people who feel they will never find another job.[3]

On average men leave the labor market earlier now than they did in the 1950s and 1960s. Often this is not a planned early retirement, but individuals forced out of work by circumstances beyond their control. Of the mature unemployed, 47% have been out of work for a year or more, compared to only 33% of the unemployed aged 18 to 24.[4] In the UK and Australia, the mature unemployed risk to be out of work twice as long as their US counterparts.

The over-50 job seeker falls into one of the most serious forms of unemployment, structural unemployment, which is usually tied to changes in the economy. Structural unemployment occurs when a person is ready and has the desire to work, yet cannot find work either because none is available or they lack the skills to be hired for existing positions. As the numbers above show, these people can potentially remain unemployed for months, perhaps years, and eventually they may drop out of the workforce all together and settle for early retirement.

In a survey taken in May 2017 by TNS Tracker Survey for Age UK, 20% of people aged 50 to 64 are concerned about being made redundant or becoming unemployed in the next six months, and 26% are worried about the security of their income over the next six months.[5] In Australia the statistics point to a similar degree of difficulty for older people trying to re-enter the workforce: 36% of unemployed men 55 to 64 years of age found themselves unemployed for over 12 months, versus 21% for males aged 15 to 24. As of June 2017 in the UK over 1.87 million people aged 50 and over work for themselves, and this number will only rise. [6]

In a nutshell, overall employment and unemployment rates show us that a vast number of mature people worldwide are working but nonetheless falling into poverty.

Underemployment and Cyclical Employment

Pick up any newspaper or watch the news on TV and you are likely to see stories about the unemployment rates in your state or country. They could be up, they could be down. There is another form of unemployment that you're likely to hear little about: underemployment. No, that is not a typo. Underemployment, also known as disguised unemployment, is when an individual is employed below their desired capacity, whether in terms of financial remuneration, number of working hours, or their level of skillset or experience.

Put another way, underemployment might mean being underpaid, but it can also mean a job that is in some important way insufficient to the worker, which results in the under-utilization of that employee. An underemployed person might work a part-time job despite wanting full-time hours. Alternatively, an underemployed person may be holding a job where they are overqualified in terms of their education, years of experience, or other skill sets.

An example of this might be when a highly skilled person has settled for working in a coffee shop or as a clerk in a retail store. While not technically unemployed, the underemployed person is often competing for available jobs in the market.

Underemployment can occur because of a recession or other change in the economy, when there are more skilled workers in the marketplace than there are jobs, because of corporate layoffs and forced early retirement, or when technological advances reduce the need for manual or skilled labor.

Another form of unemployment that flies under the radar is cyclical unemployment, which is related to the cyclical trends in industry or business cycles. When the demand for a product or service is reduced, production need is also reduced. The knock-on effect is that less labor is required, forcing companies to let employees go. When the economy bounces back the company rehires, completing the cycle.

An issue parallel to underemployment or cyclical unemployment, and one that will have repercussions for the over-50 person looking for work, is the gig economy.

Implications of the Gig Economy

New technology has facilitated the growth of the so-called gig economy and at the same time has altered the nature of the workplace in many industries. Gone is the era of the lifelong job and the financial security that went along with it. Researchers are asking, "Is the gig economy a fad?" The evidence says no.

The gig economy is the collection of markets that match providers (individuals, or gig workers) to consumers on a gig basis (by job or engagement) in support of on-demand commerce. In the basic model, gig workers enter into formal agreements with on-demand companies to provide services to the company's clients.

Prospective clients, whether companies or individuals, request services through an internet-based platform or smartphone application that allows them to search for providers or to advertise specific jobs. Gig workers are engaged by the on-demand company to provide the requested services, and are compensated for their work.[7]

In the gig economy environment temporary positions or contingent work are common and organizations contract independent workers for engagements that tend to be short-term and unpredictable work arrangements negotiated through online peer-to-peer marketplaces.[8]

A contingent workforce is a provisional group of workers who work for an organization on a non-permanent basis, with no implicit or explicit contract for long-term employment. These contingent workers—or giggers—are also known as freelancers, independent professionals, temporary contract workers, independent contractors, or consultants.[9]

Gig jobs may differ from traditional freelance jobs in a few ways. The coordination of jobs through an on-demand company reduces entry and operating costs for freelancers. It also allows workers' participation to be more transitory in gig markets, with greater flexibility around work hours.

Some companies allow freelancers to set prices or select the jobs that they take on (or both), whereas others maintain control over price-setting and assignment decisions. Some operate in local markets (e.g., select cities) while others serve a global client base.

Although driver services such as Lyft, Uber, and Sidecar and personal and household services (for example TaskRabbit and Handy) are perhaps best known, the gig economy operates in many sectors, including business and administrative services (such as Freelancer, Upwork and Fiverr), delivery services (including Instacart, Postmates), and medical care (Heal and Pager, for example).

McKinsey Global Institute, listing the main gig economy digital platforms for professional freelance work, found that Upwork (formerly Elance/Odesk) had 2.5 million registered users. There were 280,000 drivers registered with Uber, Lyft, and Sidecar and multitude of non-professional service providers operate through other sites such as TaskRabbit, not to mention Postmates, Favor, and Instacart for messengers and shoppers.

Technology plays an important role in the gig economy. The internet, smartphones, and sophisticated software mean that companies can reach a wider pool of workers than before.

In this way technology allows companies to have a large workforce on standby, ready to respond to changes in demand. This frees companies from needing to pay workers to carry out fixed shifts, which may be good for companies and consumers, but the lack of certainty can be bad for workers.[10]

In the EY Contingent Workforce Study survey of June 2016, employers in the US shared that their organizations averaged 17% contingent workers. This is not just a US phenomenon. Across the pond in the UK, a similar story is being told. Over a period of 10 years to 2016 the number of self-employed individuals has reached record highs at 4.8 million, as opposed to only 6% growth in the UK for hired employees over the same period. The story doesn't end there. Countries like the Netherlands, Belgium, France, and Australia are also witnessing similarly rapid growth in the self-employed workforce.[11]

If you're over 50 and at risk of losing your full-time job, here's where things really start to get scary. The question you need to ask yourself is whether you're at risk of losing your position because of a downturn in the economy and a company's desire to save money—or is the position being replaced by automation and technology?

Current trends in the US match those in Europe and Australia. The EY Contingent Workforce Study predicts that by 2020 almost one in five US workers will be contingent—that's roughly 31 million people.

Many see the gig economy as fundamentally changing the nature of work, with marked declines in full-time and regular employment. It's likely that more and more people will be working more than one job or will be classified as self-employed, as micro-business owners, or as freelancers.

In the absence of full-time work, many workers who opt for contingent work do so as an interim measure, yet they run the risk of this becoming a more permanent solution.

According to a 2016 report by the Work Foundation at Lancaster University, the recent acceleration in self-employment is coming from the top three highly-skilled occupational groups of managers, professionals, and associate and technical staff.[12] Between January and March of 2016 high-skill self-employment grew much faster than during the same three-month period in 2010, contributing two-thirds of the overall increase in self-employment for that three-month period.

Technological advances, including high-quality and relatively cheap broadband connections, have encouraged and facilitated the growth of freelancing. A high share of the self-employed have always worked from home, and that share has increased over time.

The term "gig economy" defies a narrow definition, but it is increasingly being used to describe people who do not work fixed shifts, who are not required to carry out a minimum number of hours per day, and who can work as much or as little as they desire. Somewhat misleadingly, the word "gig" suggests work that is casual and inessential. However, for many participants in the gig economy, this work is their main source of income.

For persons in their 50s and 60s, having to rely on the gig economy to support their families is not likely to be financially feasible unless they are entering into high-paying consultation contractual arrangements.

Finding work, be it part-time employment or other contingent gig economy work, allows over-50 individuals to maintain some form of income, but that income can look like peanuts when a single-family household of 50–60 Somethings unexpectedly becomes a three- or four-generation household, when unemployed grown children return home to live with their parents.

Welcome to the Club Sandwich Generation.

The Club Sandwich Generation and Boomerang Kids

Unless you are close to reaching your 50s it's likely you may not have heard about the Sandwich Generation or, in the case of anyone 50 and above, the Club Sandwich Generation. Heck, you might be living this right now without knowing there was a term for it.

Dorothy Miller coined the term "Sandwich Generation" in 1981 to describe adult children who are sandwiched between aging parents and their own maturing children. "Club Sandwich Generation" subsequently came into use as a term for people in their 50s and 60s with elderly parents, adult children, and grandchildren.

Additional financial challenges for the Club Sandwich Generation come courtesy of the Boomerang Generation, or Boomerang Kids. The typical Boomerang Kid is a young adult aged 25 to 34 who left the household to go to college or for work, yet ends up back home after graduation or a job loss. According to a Pew Research Center study, at least one in three young adults in the US lives with parents.[13]

More than one in five American adults act as caregivers to other adults, a figure which represents 23 million American households. Of these caregivers, nearly 90% are helping relatives. Nearly two in ten adults aged 60 and older say they have already cared for an aging family member.

Adult children are often the first in line to care for aging parents. While most are only taking care of one elderly family member, 30% care for two or more. The average duration of such caregiving is four years, and on average caregivers to an elderly family member report more than 5,500 USD annually in out-of-pocket spending.[14]

The challenges faced by the Club Sandwich Generation—that is, looking after elderly parents and their own adult children and their families—can have significant emotional, physical, and financial effects.

The financial burdens associated with caring for multiple generations are mounting, and the increased pressure is coming primarily from grown children rather than aging parents.

While some parents simply provide assistance, other parents are the primary source of financial support for their grown children. Among adults with at least one child aged 18 or older, 31% say they provide the primary financial support to one or all of their grown children. Among adults ages 40 to 59 with a grown child, 42% provide primary support. This represents a significant increase from 2005, when those providing primary support were at 33% in the same group.[15]

For some adults over 50 the financial burdens and responsibilities go both ways—they are supporting both an aging parent and helping a grown child. Some 15% of adults ages 40 to 59 are providing financial support to a parent age 65 or older, as well as either raising a minor child or supporting a grown child.[16] A job loss for a 50–60 Something responsible for multiple generations of family could come as a major blow to the entire family's well-being. One can only imagine the household dynamics if the only source of income is from a part-time job.

For the mature person who is either unemployed or underemployed and who is competing for full-time jobs replaced by the gig economy while looking after multiple generations, the world is likely to stay in state of flux for some time, given global trends toward increased longevity.

The Rise in Life Expectancy

If you're living a happy and fulfilling lifestyle, why wouldn't you want to live longer, to see more, to be more? But if you're experiencing unemployment or suddenly your income is significantly reduced, living longer may not sound like good news.

According to the Organization for Economic Co-operation and Development, older people are living longer.[17] Life expectancy—defined as the average number of years that a person can expect to live according to age-specific mortality rates prevalent in that person's country in a particular year—has increased substantially thanks to medical innovations and a variety of other factors.

Based on the Pew Research Center's findings in *Living to 120 and Beyond,* some futurists think even more radical changes are coming, including medical treatments that could slow, stop, or reverse the aging process and allow humans to remain healthy and productive to the age of 120 or more. I know—I can already hear you saying "Yikes!"

Increasing longevity presents the prospect of many years of post-retirement leisure and at the same time it introduces the possibility of spending long periods in various states of disability and poor health. Planning for retirement and old age—both in terms of lifestyle and finances—will become even more important, yet I dare say the average over-50 guy or gal on the street isn't even thinking about this. It's just not something that tends to be on the radar.

In the US, where birthrates are falling as life expectancy rises, the population is rapidly aging. According to US Census Bureau projections, by 2050 one in five Americans will be 65 or older, and at least 400,000 will be 100 or older. Life expectancy is on the rise in the UK and Australia as well.[18] In fact, Australia is one of the longest-living nations in the world.

Studies of the assets of older Australians show that many individuals, particularly women and those living in high-cost cities such as Sydney, are woefully ill prepared.[19] In addition, at a time when they are also planning for their own old age, many middle-aged Australians are struggling with caring for elderly parents who are living beyond expectation.[20]

In the UK the population has undergone a fundamental change in its age structure, with many people having fewer children and living longer lives. As a result, the average age of the UK population is increasing. In mid-2014, the average age exceeded 40 for the first time. By 2040, nearly one in seven people is projected to be aged over 75. As the population ages, so will the UK workforce.[21]

In addition, the spending strategies of many retirees may prove to be inconsistent with their true longevity prospects. Enjoying the fruits of their labor in early retirement may leave many people seriously short later on, when health and care costs will inevitably be higher.

By 2015 more than 1.6 billion people in the world were over 50 years of age, and this number is projected to double to nearly 3.2 billion people by 2050. The US alone is home to 111 million in the over-50 demographic.[22]

In 2000, Americans over 50 comprised 42% of the over-25 population; in 2013, that proportion reached 51%, and it is expected to grow to 54% by 2032. Longer life-spans will result in a consistently large over-50 population even after the Baby Boomer wave has crested.

By 2050, Gen Xers and Millennials will be part of the 50-plus community. The group of people in their 50s and 60s is projected to grow by 45% between 2015 and 2050, while the under-50 population will expand by just 13%. As a result, the older cohort will account for 40% of the population by 2050. As the size and productivity of this group increases over time, so will the economic returns.[23]

For Baby Boomers preparing for their future at age 50, the prospect of 38.8 more years of life for women and 34.4 more years for men may not be something they have fully anticipated. And for someone over 50 who becomes unemployed or underemployed and who has not prepared financially for the next half of their life, with its increased medical expenses and insurance premiums and other care costs, the promise of longevity can be extremely daunting.

It is a sobering thought that of the Baby Boomer generation, 52% of women and 34% of men of can expect to live to age 90. The question is, how prepared will they be? How prepared are you?

The idea of extended life expectancy will catch many people off guard. For those who do expect to live well into their 80s and 90s, far too many have a false sense of security, believing that they will be able to live well and maintain a comfortable lifestyle using their pension plans. This false sense of security may well turn into panic once they learn about the upwards adjustments on retirement ages being enacted around the world.

Pension Schemes and The Impending Social Security Crisis

A survey conducted by the Employee Benefit Research found that 47% of American workers have less than $25,000 set aside for retirement. A separate study found that while older workers tend to be more conscientious about setting money aside than younger ones, most of them have underestimated the actual and future costs of retirement.[24]

Many Americans think that Social Security will be enough to sustain them during their retirement. But with the sustainability of Social Security itself in question, it's time to think again.

The Status of Social Security

Signed by Franklin D. Roosevelt in 1935, the Social Security Act was originally set up simply as a retirement plan paid out to the primary worker until the law was changed, in 1939, to allow survivor benefits and benefits for the retiree's spouse and children. In 1956 disability benefits were added.

The Social Security program provides a basic level of monthly income to workers and their families once the workers have reached a specific age, become disabled, or died. The program now benefits over 50 million people and is financed with payroll taxes from over 150 million workers.

However, the financial status of Social Security funds is set to change in 2020, and Social Security may not necessary provide the safety net that many Americans are relying on for their future. Beginning in 2020, according its Board of Trustee's estimates, Social Security will begin paying out more in benefits than it generates in revenue. This will be the result of the ongoing retirement of Baby Boomers, which lowers the worker-to-beneficiary ratio, coupled with lengthening life expectancies allowing people to claim benefits for longer periods of time.[25] The recent recession and subsequent weak economy have also resulted in higher outlays and lower tax revenues for Social Security.

In other words, incoming funds will no longer offset outgoing benefits, and Social Security's capital of more than $2.8 trillion will begin to dwindle. As the cash pile shrinks, so will the interest income that is generated for the program. Higher interest rates could help offset this a bit, but not enough to prevent the program from running out of capital by 2034.[26] Once this money is gone, the Trustees have estimated that across-the-board benefit cuts of as much as 21% may be needed to sustain payouts through the year 2090.

In addition, American's poor saving habits mean they will be more reliant than ever on Social Security during retirement. Social Security benefits are a key income source for many retired Americans and for some, the only income.

Men and women over 50 who find themselves unemployed and out of options on the job front may begin tapping into their Social Security benefits a lot earlier than they planned to. And as the full retirement age continues to increase, there are greater reductions in benefits for persons who claim them before they reach full retirement age.

Full retirement age is the age at which a person first becomes entitled to full, unreduced retirement benefits. Currently that is age 66 and two months for people born between January 2, 1955 and January 1, 1956. For someone age 62 retiring in 2017, the monthly benefit amount would be reduced nearly 26%.[27]

American Baby Boomers typically rely on their company 401K retirement plans in addition Social Security benefits to fund retirement. A forced early exit from the workplace in their 50s can mean a significant reduction in 401K benefits, further destabilizing their prospects for their end-of-life years, and the over-50 unemployed might rightly begin to feel that the world is crumbling all around them.

Pension Schemes in the United Kingdom

Nearly 48% of the UK working population have not yet saved anything for retirement and have no idea of how much they will need. Another 21% are at least saving for the future through a pension, a Cash ISA (individual savings account) or by over-paying on a mortgage, yet they still don't have an idea of how much they will need, according to the Skipton Building Society's Retirement Tracker (and research carried out by YouGov). [28]

Citizens who were saving are also cited as not saving enough to maintain their current lifestyle well into retirement. Millions of employees are now resigned to working into old age, as years of record-low interest rates have taken their toll on pensioner savings. Twenty-one million people, or two thirds of the total 31.5 million UK workforce, will work beyond the current retirement age of 65.[29]

As of November 2016, 12.9 million people were receiving state pensions (retirement funds), with 46% of pensioner couples and 71% of single pensioners receiving half their income from state pensions and benefits, while 7% of pensioner couples and 24% of single pensioners have no other source of income other than their benefits.[30]

Is waiting for improved interest rates the answer, while living off state pension plans insufficient for the final three or four decades of life? I believe there is another way for 50–60 Something Britons. Keep reading.

The Predicament of Australian Retirees

A retirement study commissioned by News Corp Australia found that about 61% of workers expect to continue working past retirement age.[31]

Australia has its own schemes for providing financial support for its retirees, including the Superannuation Guaranteed Scheme (nicknamed Super) to which all Australian employers must contribute a mandatory 12% of their employees' salary. Employees can make additional contributions if they choose.

For most people, Super is not sufficient to fund a comfortable retirement, even if they have contributed to superannuation for most of their working lives. Moreover, Super accounts aren't sufficient to fund retirement for all Australians, especially low earners and people who spend time outside of the labor force.

The Age Pension co-exists with Super and is a government allowance paid to eligible Australians who have reached retirement age. The Age Pension is income- and asset-tested, which means the amount recipients are entitled to receive will depend on any other income received from paid work, Super benefits, personal investments, and assets.

From July 1, 2017, the qualifying age for the Age Pension, depending on your birthdate, will be 65 years and 6 months. After that, the qualifying age for the benefit will go up six months every two years until July 1, 2023.

People aged 60 to 64 will have reduced readiness, as they have not received the long-term benefits of the Superannuation Guarantee Scheme contributions.[32]

Couples are expected to be better off than singles, who are particularly under-prepared for retirement, being three times more likely than people in couples to have severely inadequate projected retirement incomes.

As a 50–60 Something individual in Australia, the UK, the US, or wherever you've spent your working years, will your pension provide you with the lifestyle you wish to lead for the next 30 to 40 years of your life? What is the answer for mature workers who face long-term unemployment or underemployment; the impact of the gig economy on full-time jobs; being sandwiched between multiple generations in need of care, financial assistance, or a place to live; and reduced pension funds combined with increased longevity?

How are they to weather the coming storm? In a word—entrepreneurship.

Chapter 2

Enter the 50–60™ Something Start-up Entrepreneur Paradigm Shift

If you've read through all the factors affecting the financial security of the over-50 generation, you're probably thinking that this is all just doom and gloom. There is cause for alarm, but also cause for empowerment.

Yes, I acknowledge that some people in their 50s and 60s are in for some hard times—if they choose to sit back and do nothing. They could try and scrape by with what they expect to receive from their savings, 401K plans and Social Security.

Should men and women in their 50s and 60s struggle to make ends meet, jeopardizing their current lifestyle because of social and economic factors that are out of their control? Absolutely not!

Welcome to the new employment paradigm shift. It's all about moving from the corporate workplace, military retirement, or civil service to the entrepreneurial work space. The paradigm shift is all about the 50–60 Something Start-up Entrepreneur refusing to fall victim to the 50–60 Something Poverty Economy.

It's my belief that everyone should have some form of passive income that is sizeable enough to either supplement one's current lifestyle or to cover one's daily expenses. However, the latter is not likely to be achievable for the average Joe or Jane.

What I'm advocating is if you are at risk of losing your job or you struggle because your current income is not enough to support a healthy lifestyle, then you should consider joining the 50–60 Something Start-up Entrepreneur revolution. I'm suggesting that you become an entrepreneur by choice and with a strategic plan of action, rather than jumping into entrepreneurship with a defensive mindset because your back is against the wall.

This book's premise is to help you move beyond your current work environment and into the realm of entrepreneurship as a planned, strategic transition.

Within these pages I'm going to show you how to develop a business using a step-by-step process so that you hit the ground running knowing that you have covered all elements of a business start-up, and that you have a greater chance of success from the moment you launch.

Here's What You'll Learn:

> How to find a product or service to sell by identifying the pains, problems, or needs of the market

> How to identify the exact ideal client who is experiencing the pain or problem or has a need

> What product, service solution, or system to offer based on your area of expertise or knowledge of a craft or hobby

> How to develop a brand perception that draws consumers to you like bees to honey

> How and why to review the competition's strengths and weaknesses to establish your ideal positioning in the marketplace

> How to establish your consulting fee or a pricing structure that supports a profitable business

> How to create your marketing strategy using a variety of tactics based on your objective, budget, and timeline

> ➤ How to embrace technology as your new best friend in order to save time, money, and human resources

> ➤ What tips, tools, and techniques will support your venture to help you avoid being overwhelmed as a new business owner.

It's time to get real. If you are in your late 40s, 50s, or 60s and you decide to start a business, you're going to need a head start. You don't have the benefit of time to establish a learning curve. My goal is to shorten your learning curve by getting straight to what you need, thereby helping you to avoid some of the mistakes that I made in the early days of my journey as a businesswoman.

The best scenario is for you to begin your entrepreneur start-up journey well in advance of leaving your current employment. If that's not a possibility, don't worry—you're still going to benefit enormously from the strategies in these pages, though once you get started you'll be working at a different pace and with a greater sense of urgency.

What is Entrepreneurship?

Before I dive into the nuts and bolts of building a business, I want to share my definition of entrepreneurship and why I think it is so important. In simple terms, *entrepreneurship is about solving a problem for someone else and making a profit by offering that solution.* Think about that for a moment. Your purpose is to solve another person's problem.

When you realize that your goal as a business owner is to solve a problem for someone else, you will be 10 steps ahead of your competition. I don't care what industry you are in or what type of product or service you are thinking about—you are in the business of solving a problem, taking away your client's pain, offering a solution for someone who needs it.

Another key takeaway for you to understand is that people do not buy products or services, they buy results. They are buying the benefits or the transformation they *believe* your product or service will provide them.

When I truly let that principle sink in and resonate in my mind, it changed everything about how I operated, specifically how I marketed my business.

My message was no longer fixed on the product name and what it did or what I did. My message spoke to the client's pain and how I could relieve them of that pain. My focus became the benefit—the pain relief—and the transformation, or how their life will be better without this pain.

In other words, you need to focus on selling the problem and being the solution.

I'd like you to pause here for a moment so that you can really sit with that. Think about the idea you are considering for your business. What are the benefits? What is the transformation that your client would gain by purchasing your service, system, or solution?

What Makes Me Qualified to Write a Book on Entrepreneurship?

I want to commend you for taking the first steps toward creating your new business. For some people becoming an entrepreneur is a pre-planned decision, and others will take this path out of necessity.

Within these pages I'm going to share with you eight-part process I refer to as the Entrepreneurship Path, which will demystify the basics of setting up a business, plus a few other chapters that I believe will be beneficial as you begin your journey as a business owner.

At this point you're asking yourself, "What gives her the right to tell me how to become an entrepreneur?" I'm glad you're wondering, because it gives me the opportunity to introduce myself and tell you a bit about my own entrepreneurial journey and why helping others become successful entrepreneurs is so important to me.

I've been a business owner for over 25 years now, since back in the day when people used typewriters and fax machines. When I tell young people that I've been in business for longer than some of them have been on the planet, I have the feeling they believe I started out on my own personal entrepreneurship path in a covered wagon.

So we've established that I've been doing this a while, but let me get back to answering your question. Entrepreneurship is my life and my joy, but throughout my 25 years owning several businesses, things haven't always been rosy.

I'm sure if you were to Google my name, you'd find articles I've written or events I've been a part of. It's all too easy to check out my professional record: there are not too many people out there with as Harry Potter-esque a surname as Wigglesworth.

The information out there is all the stuff you'd expect to see from someone in my line of work as a branding and marketing consultant. Some things might even get you to sit up and say "Wow!"

But that's me now. The road to success was not smoothly paved, and the name Wigglesworth didn't always yield such search results. My path, like that of any other aspiring entrepreneur, was often bumpy.

What might surprise you the most is that it was a business failure that brought me to where I am today. In 2001, due to poor sales following the 1998 financial crisis in Asia, I was forced to close my ladies' clothing boutique. The business was dying and I needed to get out of my two-year retail lease, which had just over seven months remaining. Naturally the landlords were not pleased with my decision and insisted that I pay them for the remaining months. It cost $40,000 to terminate the store lease.

Ouch! BIG OUCH! That money came mainly from my husband's personal savings, so you can only imagine the tension in the household during that time. Fortunately (if we can refer to anything in this situation as fortunate), he recognized that waiting until the lease was up to close the store wasn't going to improve the situation, and that I might be risking bankruptcy by doing so. Today, time has made it a bit easier for me to mention this financial loss without shuddering.

After the store closed, hindsight and reflection helped me to see how my lack of marketing knowledge had contributed to the demise of my business. I didn't know enough about how to get the word out about the store to bring people in and make my business thrive, or even keep it afloat. Mind you, this was way before online marketing and email broadcasts.

I knew in my heart that I wasn't finished being an entrepreneur, and that the next time I started a business, it would be different. I knew I was going to have to up my game when it came to pitching investors and suppliers. I chose to fail forward, to make that $40,000 count for something.

That business failure and financial loss became the catalyst for what I do today. You see, I'm on a mission. My mission is to empower as many over-50 individuals as I can with the entrepreneurial skills, knowledge, tactics, techniques, and strategies that will allow them to succeed in their business endeavours.

I'm on a mission to ensure that no one will have to sacrifice hard-earned savings to cover the debt of a failing business or any other expense, big or small, just because they didn't have the necessary skills to set up and operate a business.

I'm on a mission to share what I know with this group of people so that they can live their lives on their own terms, not according to the terms imposed by a company or society that says they have nothing else to contribute.

My experience as a veteran entrepreneur has also served me well in my role as a lecturer on entrepreneurship with a business school, teaching evening classes and conducting one- and two-day seminars on branding, entrepreneurship, and marketing in multiple countries.

In addition to *The 50–60 Something Start-up Entrepreneur*, I'm also the author of *Small Business Acceleration: Get Noticed Using Facebook, LinkedIn,*

Email Marketing, Public Relations and Video Marketing and *Public Relations: An Easy, Step-by-Step Guide to Creating a Public Relations Plan.*

My degree is from the School of Hard Knocks and what I share with you is designed to shorten your learning curve and accelerate your business results. Stick with me and let me show you how the entrepreneur path framework will teach you what you need to set up and run your own business. I'm here to offer my support as you become part of the start-up entrepreneur revolution.

For those corporations who are making their mature, experienced workers redundant, you have got this all wrong. For the record, as 50–60 Somethings we're just getting started.

Do You Have an Entrepreneur's Mindset?

You might have picked up this book for any number of reasons: the need for additional income as you prepare for retirement, re-entering the workplace as an empty-nester, leaving the military, or forced early retirement under one of its many guises—retrenchment, getting fired or let go, or being made redundant.

The first question you're likely to ask yourself is, "Do I have what it takes to be an entrepreneur? Can I do this?" It's a valid question to ask oneself and it's the one thing that may concern you the most, especially if you've been let go from a job.

Let's talk about that for a moment, because we tend to underestimate the effects of losing a job on one's self-esteem.

Yes, I've been there. I was let go from a job and it had nothing to do with my performance. In fact, I had received a raise just three months before I was let go.

At a San Francisco apparel company my boss and I were given separate assignments, by one of the buyers, to get patterns sent to Los Angeles by way of our in-house overnight trucks. Twice this was requested of us and twice my packages arrived, but not those of my supervisor.

When it happened the first time and the buyer reprimanded us, my boss turned to me after the buyer had walked away and said, "We screwed up." The second time this happened he said the same thing, but this time the buyer whirled around and yelled, "No, Martin, there is no *we* in this case. *You* screwed up. Pam's parcels always arrived. Yours didn't, so don't you dare include her in your screw-up!"

That was it. I knew my days were numbered because I was now the enemy. As far as my boss was concerned, I made him look bad to someone who reported directly to the vice president and owner of the company.

Three weeks later I was given the push with the remark, "It's time for us to part ways." Although I expected that this would happen, it left me feeling demotivated and unsettled nonetheless, all the more so because I knew I hadn't done anything wrong.

Even if you haven't done anything wrong and you feel the reason you were let go is unjustified, losing a job can wreak havoc on your self-esteem. Some of the emotions you might experience are:

➢ Feeling unworthy, not good enough

➢ Lack of energy

➢ Embarrassed

➢ Ashamed (this can happen even when entire departments are retrenched)

➢ Shattered or low self-confidence

➢ Feeling like it was your fault

➢ Feeling broken, like something is wrong with you

Any combination of these feelings could leave you questioning your ability to find a new job, let alone start a new business. I hear you.

While losing a job can rock your world and leave you feeling unsettled, even leaving a situation that doesn't suit you can affect your emotional stability. If you've had this experience, know that you are not alone. More importantly, know that there is nothing wrong with you.

I felt many of the emotions I've listed above when I was forced to close my women's boutique because of the Asian financial crisis of 1998. Once I closed the store, I gave myself permission to have a two-week pity-party and wallow in my feelings of shame and failure.

By the time the two weeks were up, it was time to get serious and figure out what the next chapter of my life would be. I chose to continue the path of entrepreneurship. I made the decision to fail forward.

The fact that you picked up this book and you have read this far says a lot about you. It tells me that you're most likely past the pity-party stage, that you're ready to dive back into the workplace, or that you've decided you're ready for the new career path in the next phase of your life. You are ready to take positive action.

You're reading this because you are serious about starting a business and you want to get it right from the word go, or at the very least to anticipate and reduce the inevitable bumps in the road.

Do you have what it takes to be a 50–60 Something Start-up Entrepreneur? I believe you do. Let me tell you why I believe that to be true.

Why Mature Entrepreneurs Have a High Success Rate

Today more than ever it may seem like starting young is the best way to build a successful business. After all, when you're young you have nothing to lose and a lot of energy to spend, and since your whole life is ahead of you, you can afford to make mistakes and learn from them. But starting older has its definite advantages. In fact, it turns out that for many people, starting a business in their 50s is even better than starting young. Yep, you read that correctly.

Some of the world's best known and most profitable businesses were started by entrepreneurs over 50. Pharmacist and physician John Pemberton was 55 when, in an effort to create an alternative to morphine, removed the "French Wine" from his French Wine Coca recipe and founded Coca-Cola. Colonel Harland David Sanders was 65 when he opened a small service station and started working with franchises, establishing what would later become one of the world's best-known fast-food brands: KFC.

You might say, "That was then, but things have changed." To some extent things have changed, in that it's now easier than ever for anyone to become an entrepreneur and start a business, which is why so many entrepreneurs are starting young. But here are some current facts to inspire anyone over 50 to start a business.

> Entrepreneurs over 55 are almost twice as likely to build successful businesses than entrepreneurs aged 20 to 34. This is true even for the highly competitive tech industry, where young entrepreneurs are thought to have a head start because they grew up with the internet and 21st century technology.

> Small business activity rates in the United States in the last 10 years were dominated by entrepreneurs aged 55 to 64. There are many reasons for this, including a new approach to retirement that technology and modern life makes possible, strong professional connections, and the ease with which almost anyone can start a business.

> Start-ups that survive are more likely to be led by owners over 45 years of age, according to a study, carried out by the Kauffman Ewing Institute, which followed five thousand start-ups from 2004 to 2008. No less than 64% of the surviving start-ups were led by older entrepreneurs.

> People over 50 years of age have a greater potential to create innovative companies, products, and solutions. This may surprise you, but the capacity to innovate increases with age and practice. Whether you want to create a start-up in an industry you know well or start afresh pursuing a passion in a new industry, the experience that comes with being over 50 can be a big advantage.

> People over 55 years are more likely to launch a high-growth start-up than those under 35. This trend is general, not limited

to specific industries. Older entrepreneurs have the experience, skills, and insight necessary to guide their venture to success. They can better manage fears and expectations and they have the balance and determination to persist in spite of obstacles.

Consider all these findings together and the message is simple: being 50 or older is not only *not* an obstacle to becoming an entrepreneur, but it also increases your chances of achieving success. While this insight won't eliminate challenges or make building your start-up any easier, it can be a wonderful incentive for you to finally create the business you always wanted to have.

Laying the Foundation for Entrepreneurship

It's time to get busy. You are ahead of the curve now that you know what's in store for individuals in their 50s and 60s, and you've established that you have an entrepreneur mindset. Now it's time to roll up your sleeves and create your business.

The next chapters of this book are focused on the Entrepreneurship Path Framework, which consists of eight elements: *pain, person, product, perception, positioning, price, place, and platform.* I will introduce these elements in a specific order designed to help you lay the foundations that will enable you to start your business—and then to run it.

The last three chapters of the book, once we've explored the Entrepreneurship Path Framework, are also important to your success. In these chapters I'll discuss topics new business owners can find intimidating because they feel daunted by the implementation of certain sales and technology strategies.

Starting a new business can be extremely rewarding and at the same time it can be a very lonely experience. You might find that you don't know where or who to turn to for assistance. The final chapter of this book will give you some landmarks to steer by when you're feeling overwhelmed, and will help you know where to seek support.

In joining the 50–60 Something Entrepreneur movement you'll discover a host of men and women just like you, ready to be your cheerleaders and to boost you on your journey. Consider me your first cheerleader and biggest fan.

As John Wayne said in *The Cowboys*, "Hurry up, we're burning daylight."

Chapter 3

Pain: What is the Prospect's Problem?

When you picked up this book with the notion of becoming an entrepreneur, you may or may not have had an idea of what you wanted to do. When you Google *how to start a business*, the other top search request is, *what kind of business should I start?*

There are people in the world who have always dreamed of starting their own business. Some knew what they wanted to do, while others knew only that they wanted to experience the freedom of business ownership even if they didn't know exactly what that business would look like. Then there are others who never aspired to become an entrepreneur and have opted to go down this road for a variety of reasons: to create a new lifestyle, create a new primary source of income, or add a secondary revenue stream.

If the idea of stepping into entrepreneurship is new to you, then of course the question of what to do is a big one. How you get to the place of deciding to be an entrepreneur is irrelevant. What matters most is what you are going to do. What will your business be all about?

You're on the starting line, ready to take the first step on the entrepreneurship path: identifying the consumer's pain or problem.

It All Starts With a Need

We've already established that entrepreneurship is about solving a problem for someone and making a profit. As an entrepreneur, you'll first want to identify a problem, a desire, a pain, or a need in the marketplace.

This is a key point to understand, so don't skip over it even if you already have an idea of what you want your product or service to be. Trust me, it's going to be a lot easier for you to promote your new product or service if it corresponds to an existing need, if it's the solution people are already looking for. Make sure you're not attempting to sell something no one wants.

Have you ever attended a trade show or fair and noticed that there are always certain booths that no one is visiting? Take a closer look and you'll probably conclude it's because no one needs what they're offering. They are exhibiting at a trade show because their mates, their colleagues, or their mom told that what they created is wonderful.

Rule number one: don't listen to your mom. Or better yet, listen to your mom but keep in mind that because she loves you she's always going to tell you what you've done is great, even if it sucks.

When it comes to thinking about a business, the first question to ask is, what problem can you solve for other people? Where is there a need in the market? What is already being offered by others, and could you do it better or differently? Perhaps your own unfulfilled needs have helped you identify a gap in the market.

Is it possible for you to create a brand new product or a service that is not currently available in the market? Yes, that is possible, but creating the desire, the interest, and the need will not be easy. It could potentially be a hard sell.

Did you know that you needed—or even wanted—"1000 songs in your pocket" when Steve Jobs introduced the iPod? None of us did, and yet it was a huge success. Steve Jobs knew the need existed before the consumer did. The iPod was also successful because Apple had their brand name and a huge marketing budget behind them.

I am not saying that you shouldn't start by creating an original and innovative product or service. However, be fully aware that it will take more time, more effort, and greater resources behind to create the buzz you'll need to sell your offering if you need to persuade consumers of a need they don't already know they have.

My goal here is not to be a buzz-kill, so if the business idea that's been stewing in your mind is going to be perfect for a target market you've already identified, then go for it. I'll be happy that you proved me wrong.

What Problem Should You Solve?

Many new business owners leave the corporate world to offer the same type of service under their own banner. When I started my first business, l left a job as an apparel-sourcing agent at a multi-million-dollar buying office and set up my own sourcing company. I was serving smaller companies who were unable to take advantage of the "big boy" companies that handled the high-volume orders—same industry, different target audience.

If you choose to keep practicing within an industry where you have experience, then you are already know the pain or problem of your prospective clients.

Perhaps you've been dabbling in a hobby or developing a passion for some time, selling your products and services on the side. Now that you want to take that idea to market as a full-time business, keep in mind that it must fulfill a need or solve a problem.

I cannot stress this enough. Regardless of what you plan to offer, be it product or service, solution or system, you need to solve a problem. You are fooling yourself if you think people will buy from you just because they like you personally, and because *you* think it's the best widget ever. People buy to fulfill a need, to satisfy a desire, to solve a problem, or to overcome a pain.

Now grab a pen and paper and go through the Start-up Action Steps at the end of this chapter to see what ideas come to you for your future business. Don't expect to have an idea instantaneously drop into your lap. These questions are designed to simply prompt ideas.

Start-up Action Steps

1. Think of your ideal client. What is the problem that keeps this person up at night?

2. What's the pain that they're experiencing because of this problem?

3. What are they thinking?

4. What are they worried about?

5. How does this problem affect them emotionally and physically?

6. Describe how these prospects would feel if they weren't going through this problem and pain. In other words, what do they aspire to in their lives?

7. Write out in two to three sentences the pain and problem your prospect is going through and then list the benefits and transformation that the prospect will gain from your product or service. Remember, people buy solutions to their problems, not the product or service per se.

Chapter 4

Person: Who Needs the Solution You Provide?

Now that you've worked your way through the Start-up Action Steps at the end of the last chapter, you might be generating ideas about the type of business you wish to set up. Keep letting these ideas flow.

When it comes to setting up a business, most people start with the product or service that they will offer and some even have a general idea who they will sell it to.

If you are one of those entrepreneurs moving from the corporate world and planning to do the same type of work and service the same type of clients, then you are off to a good start. Don't rush away just yet, though, as you'll still benefit from the discussion to follow.

Alternatively, you may be thinking about doing the same type of service but with a totally different target audience in mind. In this case it's important that you keep reading.

If you are completely new to entrepreneurship, this chapter will help you to get crystal clear on who your ideal client is. This is the second element in the entrepreneur path process and it will set the stage for what you offer, how you will determine your price, and where you will promote your brand. The second element in the entrepreneurship path is all about the person who has the need.

I've been living in Asia for over 27 years, both in Hong Kong and Singapore. Many of the start-up entrepreneurs or wannabe business owners I speak to want to target China as their market. I often hear statements like, "If I could just tap two percent of the Chinese market, I'd be a multi-millionaire." At the time of this writing, China's population stands at over 1.3 billion people.

When people make statements like the one above, it's clear they have no concept of what a target market means. What they've failed to understand is that not everyone is their customer. Just because a country has a huge population doesn't mean you're going to strike it rich, nor does it mean that all those people—or any of them—want what you offer.

Let's get something clear right now:

When you try to be everything to everyone, you are nothing to no one.

To be successful in business, you must clearly identify who your ideal client is and market to that person.

What I'm about to say may seem a bit harsh, but it is the truth. Your ideal client is someone who is in need, who wants your product, and who can pay for it.

As a business owner I had my share of struggles, trying to understand the marketing process without the guidance of a mentor. Once I understood what marketing was and how essential it is to have a marketing strategy and not just tactics, I was drawn to help other small business owners arrive at that understanding with less difficulty.

I decided that entrepreneurs and small business owners were the clients that I wanted to work with. The problem was, they couldn't afford to pay me—or rather they were so stuck in survival mode that they were unable to see the value of my services and therefore couldn't justify paying for the help they so badly needed.

I understand where these people were coming from because I was once in their shoes. There were many times when I knew that a consultant or software program could really help me, yet the fee or cost was prohibitive for me. I would identify what I needed and then once it was outside of my financial comfort zone, the first thing out of my mouth was, "Oh no, that's expensive, I can't afford it."

It wasn't until years later, when I started to make money in my business, that I had a major mindset shift and began to seek out ways to take my business to the next level, as I still do to this day.

The shift came when I looked into hiring a marketing consultant to help me grow my business. The fee for her services was in the thousands. My initial reaction was the well-worn tape in my head, "That's expensive, I can't afford it." Instead I choose to look at the value and the transformation that would take place in my business. If working with her could double my business, then the investment would be a drop in the bucket. I signed a contract and went for it.

Two things happened for me with this shift. One is that I no longer look at things solely from the standpoint of how much they cost but also in terms of what it costs for me to gain big results.

The second *aha* moment came when I realized that entrepreneurs and small business owners might not be hiring me because I was ineffectively communicating the value of my consulting services. I was not demonstrating the results and transformation they would achieve through working with me. The failure to inspire was all mine; I was not articulating how their lives and businesses would be better after working with me.

Let me go back to my statement about finding the ideal consumer who can pay for your services. Many people will want what you have, yet they'll tell themselves they can't afford it. The key for you is to clearly and concisely communicate your value, the benefits and transformation you bring, so that they realize that the truly need your service. If you do this effectively they will *find a way* to afford it. Anyone experiencing great pains or problems in life or business will be looking for relief. People will pay to relieve their pains and problems.

Before you even begin to set up a business, you must first identify the pain in the market and the person who is experiencing that pain. The more you focus on a specific niche the better.

Could I have written a book on entrepreneurship for any person looking to start a business? Yes, but I wanted instead to identify a niche group of people with a specific problem or need, and then provide a solution for that problem. That is how the *50–60 Something Startup Entrepreneur* came about. You are my peeps.

I also want to point out that the more specific your target audience is, the easier it is going to be for you attract the attention of your ideal clients, to get yourself in front of them where they tend to gather.

Now that you understand the importance of identifying your ideal target audience, it's time to break this down even further by establishing the demographics of that audience.

Identify the Demographics of the Target Audience

To truly know who it is you're going to serve with your business, you'll want to create a profile of your ideal client. This means identifying the demographics, or statistical characteristics, of your target audience, including age, gender, education, and household income. You'll also want to consider the psychographics, or psychological profile, of your target audience—their lifestyle, hobbies, religion, attitudes, and inspirations.

Now grab your notebook pen or pencil. Find a quiet place to write and answer the questions in the following Start-up Action Steps to get to know your ideal client.

Start-up Action Steps

1. What is the age group of your ideal target audience?

2. What is the gender of the audience?
   Male, female, or both?

3. What is the marital or relational status of this person?

4. Do they have children?

5. What is the household income?

6. What is their highest level of education?

7. Where do they live—city, suburbs, or rural area?

8. What are their hobbies or interests?

9. Why should they buy from you and not your competitor?

10. What are their values?

11. Who is *not* your target customer?

Chapter 5

The Product: How Your Service Offer Relieves the Prospect's Pain

In the previous chapters you learned how to identify the pain or problem that motivates your prospect, or target audience, to seek relief. In this chapter it's time to get into the meat and potatoes of entrepreneurship: your offer. This is the product, service, solution, framework, or system that will solve the problem and take away the pain that a person or company is going through.

Before we get into the actual type of product or service you'll be offering, you will need to look at two very important factors that will define everything you do from this point forward—your desired lifestyle and your business model.

What Kind of Lifestyle Do You Desire?

About seven years ago I heard an expression that I wish I had encountered at the start of my entrepreneurial journey. I'm going to share it with you here because I believe it will make a huge difference in how you develop your future business.

"Architect your life, then architect your business."

Man, I wish someone had told me that before I started writing business plans. I got so good at designing and developing business models that I completely left myself and my life out of the picture.

I'll never forget the romantic wedding-anniversary dinner with my husband in Bali, under the stars next to the ocean, when he said, "It's been another great year together. Do you think that this next year you can find more time for me amongst all your work and projects?"

He was right. My life revolved around the business and I gave other people and social activities the brush-off in the name of putting my business first. Sadly, I was doing this to my husband as well, declining outings together because I was fixated on getting my business to the next level. Not only had I ignored my family and friends, I was ignoring myself. I never made time for self-care, downtime, or indulging in my own needs. I used the excuse of not having time to exercise because it would mean taking time away from my work.

I failed to see that it didn't make any sense to have a successful business if I wasn't making time to share the fruits of my labor with the key people in my life. Furthermore, if I wasn't healthy, I wouldn't be able to sustain working at this pace, and I couldn't enjoy holiday activities without feeling worn out.

Please do yourself the biggest favour and architect the life you want to have first, then create the business around the life you want. Don't try to squeeze your life in around your business. You'll thank me for this advice later.

Do Some Soul Searching

To help you plan the kind of life you want to lead, here are a few questions for you to consider. Find a quiet place and give these important questions some thought.

- ➢ Does your current lifestyle bring you joy and contentment? Do you want to continue living the way you live now? What business model would provide your desired annual revenue and allow you to maintain a comfortable lifestyle?

- ➢ If you are looking to change your lifestyle, what does that look like? Where would you live? How many hours per week do you want to work? What would it cost to have the lifestyle you desire?

- ➢ How much capital will be required to set up and maintain the business? How long will it take you to start turning a profit? How soon do you need to be up and running?

- ➢ If you are considering this as a sideline business, what type of business would allow you to have a full-time job and run a business and maintain your family life?

- ➢ How many people rely on the income that will be generated with this business?

- ➢ Do you have the discipline to run a business? Are you able to keep your head down and keep working while your friends and family might be out having a good time? Will you be able to keep going when you face uncomfortable and challenging moments?

- ➢ Do you have the support of family and friends for the new business?

- ➢ Will your business involve a product, necessitating a different level of capital than a service-based business model would, and possibly a place to store the product?

- ➢ Do you want to buy into a readymade turnkey business such as a franchise or MML?

- ➢ Do you want to build the business from the ground up?

- ➢ What does retirement look like for you? What city will you live and in, and in what type of accommodation? How much will you need to take care of any critical care needs? How much discretionary income will you need to have the high quality lifestyle you so desire?

Grab a piece of paper and let these questions help you gain some clarity about your lifestyle and what changing it or maintaining it would mean for your business plan. Then you'll be ready to ask yourself what type of business would be compatible with the ideal lifestyle you've outlined for yourself and your family.

Just let that thought marinate in your mind for a while. You don't need to know the answer right this minute. Just allow thoughts and ideas to pop into your head, and eventually the right offer will reveal itself.

Now that you've taken a bit of time to answer the questions above and have a clearer idea of what you want your lifestyle to be in the future, it's time to look at business structure. This is key given that people today are likely to live well into their 80's and 90's.

What Type of Business Do You Want?

Several different terms can be used to describe a business entity. For the 50–60 Something Start-up Entrepreneur, we are going to be looking at *enterprise* vs. *company*.

Knowing the type of business you want to set up is the next big decision to make. An enterprise business tends to be one person running the entire operation, alone or with minimal or outsourced help. The owner of an enterprise is responsible for calling all the shots, whereas persons involved in a company setup will at some point answer to shareholders and face inquiries into finances and operations.

An enterprise is always for profit, whereas a company can be for profit or nonprofit. An enterprise can be an entirely individually-owned venture, and therefore not subject to corporate governance laws. This type of business is often referred to as a sole-proprietorship.

An enterprise is a business-oriented organization created specifically to allow the founder(s) to attract customers, sell goods and services, and earn a profit. A company is commonly defined as any commercial establishment run to earn profits for the shareholders and the owners. In a company, you sell shares of the company to others, who now have a stake in your company and therefore a share in the profits.

The easiest and cheapest way to start a business is to become a sole proprietor. Setting up a company is a bit more complicated and involves rules of governance that must be adhered to as well as the higher costs associated with maintaining the business entity.

You will need to decide what is best for you. I've owned a sole-proprietorship business, a limited liability partnership, and a private limited company. It comes down to what you want to do and offer and whether you want to have the investment benefits but also the accountability that comes with shareholders, or if you prefer to be a one-person operation.

It's best that you check what type of business entities are available in your resident country and familiarize yourself with the rules and regulations for each. A good entrepreneur does his or her due diligence.

What Does This Mean For You?

By now you've taken some time to think about what you want for yourself and your family, how you want to live, where you want to live, how many hours a day, a week that you want to work. These are all key things to consider before you sit down to craft your business. Remember, you are architecting your life and your business at the same time. Do what is right for you.

Let's move on to the different types of business models to consider.

Business Models

The types of businesses that you can start are varied and it would be impossible for me to cover them all. The best way for me to serve you, as you consider what type of business to set up, is to share an overview of a few business models for you to review. Chances are that within these descriptions you'll find a model that piques your interest and resonates with what you've already outlined as your lifestyle goals for yourself and your family as well as your objectives for the business.

Traditional Business: Goods and Services

A traditional business is typically one that you start yourself from scratch, such as an apparel business, consultancy, restaurant, accounting firm, or law practice.

In this business model you have complete control, from the onset, over every aspect of the business, including the look and feel of a retail operation, the branding, the marketing, and the people you hire to support the business. In a traditional business model, the business owner receives the net profits of the business.

If you are considering manufacturing and selling a physical product, either online or in a storefront, then you'll be deploying either the retail or wholesale business model. The retail model means that you, as manufacturer or producer, sell your product directly to the consumer. The same thing applies if you are selling a service solution.

In wholesaling, you are the manufacturer/producer and you typically sell your product in bulk quantities to a middleman or distributor, who in turn sells it to consumers. When selling as a retailer, you generally sell your product at a higher price per unit than you would as a wholesaler. Distributors buying in bulk will want to buy the product at a discount and then create their own markups.

There is much to think about when it comes to manufacturing your own goods for retail. A word to the wise: secure your orders first, with purchase orders, *before* going into production. Putting money out yourself to manufacture the product will significantly affect your cash flow. If you are dealing in seasonal goods and not all your goods sell, your cash flow will be tied up in product that doesn't move. I speak from experience; at one point in time I had $92,000 worth of merchandise (at cost) sitting in a warehouse, ready for retail. That's a hell of a lot of money to be tied up in product.

When I had a kids' golf apparel business, we started selling directly to retailers, offering them wholesale prices. Dealing with distributors was particularly advantageous, as they bought in bulk. Our big challenge was working with small retail golf pro shops who wanted to purchase fewer units due to limited space.

At the same time, we were selling at a higher retail price on our website and on Amazon. After two years we dropped the wholesale stream and continued operating strictly as an online retailer. Our profits were significantly higher once there was no middleman to deal with, and parents tended to purchase more than one item at a time, which further bumped up the profits.

Having experienced owning both service-based and retail- and wholesale-based businesses, I'd be hard pressed to start another business where I held inventory. For me, not having to worry about inventory lowers operational costs and makes service-based businesses far more profitable.

Drop Ship Retail

Fast forward to a new way of operating a retail business without any product, as an online retailer with drop shipping. Drop shipping is a retail method where a store doesn't keep the products it sells in stock, partnering instead with a wholesale supplier who stocks the product.

When you sell a product as an online retailer, the purchase happens on your website, an order is triggered for the third-party supplier, and the merchandise is shipped directly to the customer. You as merchant never see or handle the product. You need not worry about the fulfillment or inventory status. Now that's my kind of business model.

It's easy to get started, and very little capital is required. Once your website is up and running with your payment gateway and wholesale partners on board, you can literally operate from anywhere in the world as long as you have an internet connection.

This business model, like any other, has its pros and cons. As convenient as the drop ship model might be, the margins tend to be low, especially if you are offering products in a very competitive drop-shipping niche. Go back to our first chapter on pain and solving a need and then zero in on that target market's needs.

The bigger issue is finding reputable fulfillment companies to work with. Doing business this way is more mainstream than it was, say, 10 years ago, so there are some good companies out there. Ecommerce Platforms out of the UK has put together a list of top drop shipping suppliers. Their top five names include Oberlo, Doba, Salehoo (from New Zealand), Alibaba (out of China) and Worldwide Brands. Google their names along with the term *drop shipping* and you're bound to find them.

Although drop shipping may offer an easier solution for securing and listing products, as a business owner you will still need to do your research before you dive in.

All in all, this business model offers the opportunity to get into business relatively quickly, with only the small investment of setting up a website or blog and the payment gateway. This would be a great option for someone looking to run a business from home.

Buying a Franchise

Depending on your financial situation and how quickly you want to get in to a business, another possibility to consider is buying a franchise business. With this model rather than creating a business from scratch, a person or group of people start an enterprise by buying into an established, proven business.

In this model the franchisor, or owner of the original business, grants the franchisee a license to operate under a particular name or trademark within a specified territory or location and for the term agreed upon in the licensing agreement.

In addition to paying an upfront franchise fee and ongoing royalties based on a percentage of unit sales, you must agree to run the business according to the operations manual and the franchise contract. The average franchise fee ranges from 25,000 to 35,000 USD, although some franchise fees can be well over 100,000 USD.[33]

A franchise might be a good way for a newbie entrepreneur to get started because you can follow an established and successful business blueprint. The initial training, short time to opening, and ongoing support this model provides make for a higher chance of success than in a sole proprietorship.

A franchise also provides the benefits of lower cost, thanks to group purchasing, and lead generation through websites as well as national and regional advertising campaigns.

Buying an Existing Business

Another way of getting into business quickly is to buy an existing business, and thereby avoid starting from scratch. There are both advantages and disadvantages to buying a business, pros and cons that you must weigh carefully, so it's important to do your due diligence. What you think might be wonderful on the surface could be a nightmare once you get behind the scenes. Start with finding out why the owner is selling and then continue asking questions.

One of the advantages of buying an established business is that such key elements as location, equipment, and employees are already in place. More importantly, an established business already has customers who are likely to continue utilizing the business.

Because it's an existing business, the need for the product or service has already been established and it might be easier to obtain financing, if you need it, based on the proven track record of the business.

The downside of buying an existing business is the large capital investment it requires up front. Part of your due diligence will be to have an accountant go through the books to determine if the business has been profitable and, if possible, speak with the owner's bankers. Ascertain whether the business has any outstanding debts that could potentially be passed onto you.

If purchasing an existing business is the path you are considering as your business model, here are a few key questions to ask yourself when looking at a potential business for sale.

- Is the existing merchandise included in the purchase? If so, review the inventory to see if it is still viable and not aged or outdated.

- Why is this business for sale?

- What is the outlook for the future of this business given the economy, the location of the business, and the state of the merchandise and/or equipment?

- What is the current marketing plan? How are customers typically drawn in?

- How long have the employees been with the business and are there any key individuals who might be hard to replace if they choose not to stay on?

- Is it likely that big-box competitors might open nearby anytime soon, and how would that affect your business?

Overall, it's up to you to carefully do your homework and to do it with gusto. If things look too good to be true, they usually are.

Direct Sales, Network Marketing, and Multi-level Marketing

Unless you've been living under a rock, you've probably heard of this next business model, or perhaps you know of someone who is part of a company that uses this method—network marketing, also known as direct sales, multi-level marketing (MLM), or referral marketing. Network marketing employs a distributor network two or more tiers deep to build the business.

Some well-known examples of MLM businesses include Amway, Pampered Chef, Avon, Tupperware, Mary Kay, World Ventures, Herbalife, NuSkin, Doterra, and Partylite, just to name a few. If you live in the US, chances are that you have attended a Tupperware party or a Partylite get-together or that someone has invited you to "share the opportunity" of any one of these business ventures.

I admit it, I once sold Avon, and I've been to more than one Pampered Chef "Girls' Night Out" event complete with demonstrations of the cooking gear and gadgets along with food tastings. Truth be told, I still have some of those expensive gadgets in my kitchen drawers right now.

This type of direct sales business tends to be very popular with people who are already working and are looking for part-time supplemental income as well as those looking for a flexible part-time business.

Direct marketing companies tend to require a low upfront investment for the purchase of the starter kit, making it easy for you to reach out to family and friends and other personal contacts as your first customers. These companies also ask you to recruit other sales representatives who then become your "downline"—that is, their sales generate income for you and the people above you.

Each MLM company dictates its own specific compensation plan for the payout of any earnings to their respective participants. In theory these compensation plans pay out from the following two potential revenue streams.

The first form of compensation is from commissions of sales made directly by the participants to their own retail customers. The second kind of compensation is paid out from commissions based on the downline sales made by the network of distributors recruited into the MLM by the participant.

In addition to the low upfront investment, one advantage of such a business is that it offers a proven system for you to tap into while you learn and grow your business. A reputable network marketing program should include business tools, training, and teamwork to support your goals.

Once again, you must do your due diligence. Network marketing programs are usually exempt from business opportunity regulation and, since they aren't defined franchises, they don't fall under the regulation of state and federal franchise laws either.

Affiliate Marketing

With the affiliate marketing model, you as the business owner earn pre-determined commissions by promoting or other companies' products or services. There are many products and services to choose from, and the advantage of affiliate marketing is that you don't have to invest time and money developing those products or services yourself. You can get started as soon as you create a platform from which to sell, such as a blog, website, newsletter, Facebook page, or other platform, and it is possible to earn a nice living through affiliate marketing.

When you become an affiliate of a product, service, or brand, you will be assigned a unique tracking URL for each item you promote. This allows the merchant to track the traffic you send to their site.

Your role as the affiliate is to promote the product, within the rules and regulations of the brand, by reviewing it, writing about it in a blog post, or listing it on your website as a recommended resource. Your affiliate link is placed within the write-up, blog post, or product image.

When someone makes a purchase after your listed link or hyperlinked image leads them to the merchant's page, you earn a commission from that sale. Commission payments are made either by the merchant company or through an affiliate network. I would suggest working with an affiliate network as they are set up to do all the tracking of sales and are punctual about making payments according to a schedule or dollar threshold.

Worldwide there are many affiliate networks representing a multitude of products. To promote physical products you can consider Amazon Associates, CJ Affiliate by Conversant (formerly Commission Junction), Rakuten LinkShare (formally just LinkShare), SharASale, and of course eBay. There are a lot more out there, yet these are the ones that tend to rank in the top 10. If digital products are more up your alley, then you can consider Clickbank and JVZoo.

Some of these networks charge a small administration fee while others are free. I think that Amazon Associates is by far the easiest to get started with, and requires no setup or admin fee. As I mentioned, you will need to set up the sales platform where you will be promoting the affiliate products and/or services. It is important that you do this first, as each of the networks you affiliate yourself with will ask you to give the URL of a website, blog, or Facebook page.

By signing up with Amazon Associates, you can promote anything that Amazon sells on their site. You can recommend and promote books, cosmetics, cameras, baby items, crockery—you name it and you're likely to find it on Amazon as an item to be promoted as part of your business.

With each of these networks you will need to check the terms and conditions to find the commission percentages, payment terms, and which networks offer support materials like banners ads and text links.

Getting into affiliate marketing can be quick in terms of setup, but it takes time and effort to build your business and make money. If immediate cash is what you're looking for, this might not be the business model for you. Digital products tend to bring a higher commission rate than other items, yet you will still need to wait to go through a payment cycle or reach a payment threshold before you realize any cash.

Affiliate marketing is a great business model to generate passive income, so it might be particularly worth considering as something you put in place in addition to another revenue source.

What If You Don't Know What to Offer?

If you start a Google search with *what type of . . .* before you even finish entering the phrase, Google automatically offers up, *what type of business should I start?* as the first suggestion. That question gives 329,000,000 search results.

I bring this up because I don't want you to feel like you're the only person wondering what you should do when it comes to setting up a business. It's a legitimate question to be asking yourself, especially if you are considering launching a business that is different from your current or previous line of work.

If you are still unsure as to what you should be offering, then you need to go back to the issue of the target audience pain points and the notes you made using the action steps at the end of Chapter 3. What do they desire? What causes them pain? What are the problems from which they seek relief? What are they struggling with at work, at home, in life? What do they wish was available that doesn't currently exist in the marketplace?

As I always tell newbie entrepreneurs, Google is your BFF. Go get cozy with Google and type in search terms like, *how to start a business, top business ideas for the year, work from home business ideas, how to start an online business,* etc. You get the idea. Spend some quality time doing your research and jot down the things that pique your interest.

You Don't have to Reinvent the Wheel

One day a gentleman made a comment on a blog post I'd written about the success of over-50 entrepreneurs. He said he liked what he had read and then remarked that he now needed to find the next "big idea" that would allow him to start a business.

I mention him here because my response to him forms the essence of this section on your product or service offering. No your product, service, or solution does *not* have to be the next big idea to be the basis of a successful business.

You don't need to spend hour upon hour trying to come up with some new widget—the answer is much simpler. You find a product or service that meets the needs of your target audience *and* allows you to make a profit while leading the lifestyle you've mapped out for yourself.

To conclude this chapter, let me remind you again of the definition of entrepreneurship:

Entrepreneurship is about solving a problem for someone else and making a profit by offering that solution.

Whew! Take a break, then come back, jump in, and check out your Start-up Action Steps for this chapter.

Start-up Action Steps

1. What type of product, service, solution or system would relieve your ideal client of his or her problem?

2. What is the cost of acquiring your product or service for distribution to the consumer?

3. If you're purchasing or developing a product, are there minimum quantities required by the supplier?

4. What are the lead times for acquiring your product
   supplies or developing the service or system?

5. What are your prospect's priorities (ease of use,
   efficiency, saving time or money)?

6. What makes your product or service offering unique?
   What is your competitive advantage?

7. Why should they buy from you and not your
   competitor?

8. What might be some possible objections to doing
   business with you? Such objections might include,
   a) they perceive you as a new business and therefore
   as a high-risk business, b) your location is not
   conducive to doing business with you, c) your
   fee is outside their allocated budget, d) they may
   not be interested in working with a consultant of
   your gender, or e) your marketing materials look
   amateurish and don't instill trust in your business.

Chapter 6

Perception: Creating a Brand People Want

Are you familiar with the expression "perception is reality?" Peoples' perception—their belief—is their reality. Because your prospect's perception of your brand is their reality, it is important for you to be the driver, the creator as it were, of how people perceive your brand, your product, or your service offering.

Perception? You may be thinking, what does perception have to do with me becoming an entrepreneur or starting a business? In a word, everything. Perception is the forth element on the entrepreneurship path.

Branding is based on the principles of perception and its objective is to satisfy the wants and needs of the consumer. It's about communicating your message to the consumer more effectively so they immediately associate your business with their needs and desires.

As a start-up entrepreneur, your goal in the setup stage is to create a brand perception that resonates with your target market. Your objective is to create a perceived knowledge about your product or service so that when the consumer, when ready to buy, thinks about you. In a nutshell, branding is influencing your ideal clients' perceptions in a way that spurs them to action, that gets them to raise their hands and say, "That's for me, I need that!"

Don't be intimidated if the idea of creating brand perception seems difficult. When you catch on to how this is done, you'll easily be able to do it for any business that you choose to create.

How is Perception Created?

Perception is the process by which we receive information, through our five senses, and assign meaning to it. Businesses are built on customer relationships, and brand perception sets the tone for those relationships. Your brand is made up of the hundreds of perceptions that serve to create an emotional connection with your consumers.

For example, visual clues like the color pink and a script font on letterhead or advertisements can create the perception of a female-owned business or one that caters to women.

People don't buy products or services, they buy results. A woman buys facial soap not because she wants a clean face, but for the results she believes it will bring her. That could be soft, radiant, clear skin. The soap manufacturer Lux, for example, does everything possible to create the perception that a woman using Lux products desires soft, radiant and beautiful skin as a result.

Everything about the packaging contributes to the perception that Lux is for a woman who wants to have radiant skin. The brand name suggests luxury, the pastel colors signal that this product is conceived for a woman's skin, and the image of a beautiful woman with flawless, whitened skin appeals to the prospect's desire to see herself—and be seen—as beautiful, and to feel attractive and confident. This is all done very purposefully to create a perception about the product and to use the consumer's desires and aspirations to motivate a purchase.

Let's look at how these branding strategies translate to a service business. Say you own a small one- or two-person public relations company. Rather than refer to yourselves as a one-man-band operation, you could refer yourself a boutique PR agency. The word *boutique* implies intimate, sophisticated, and high-end service. In consumer perception, smaller business size can be positioned to suggest greater attention to detail. With the right branding, prospects will believe they will receive more attention, superior service, and better results with you than they would with a large firm.

The Most Important Element of Brand Perception

This leads me to the first element—and the one I believe to be the most important when it comes to creating your brand perception—the brand name.

Individual product names and pricing also play into overall brand perception. What comes to mind when you read the words Häagen-Dazs? If you're like me, your mouth is now watering at the thought of your favorite flavor of ice cream.

Häagen-Dazs has established itself as a premium brand of ice cream, sorbets, and frozen yogurt. Most people assume from the name that it is a European brand, yet it was developed in the Bronx, New York. By creating a unique name, using only the finest ingredients, and selling their original three flavors of ice cream in pint-sized packaging at a premium price, Reuben and Rose Mattus created the perception of a premium-quality, international brand of ice cream.

According to Al Ries and Jack Trout, who wrote *Positioning: A Battle for Your Mind,* "In this positioning era, the single most important decision you can make is what to name the product." [34] I couldn't agree more.

That book was first published in 1981 and has subsequently been updated, yet it remains relevant today, in particular in its guidance on brand names. Your company name is the first thing people are going to see or hear about your brand so it is vital that you get it right.

I'm going to share with you some of the poorly chosen brand names that I have come across during my mentoring sessions over the years, but before I share these brand names and the criticism I would offer about them, I'm first going to rat myself out with an example from my own learning curve.

One of the biggest mistakes I made with my second business, Seaside Clothing, was to give it about 30 minutes' worth of thought—if that—when it came to deciding the company name. In the apparel manufacturing business, no production starts on a garment unless the factory has the label on hand since that's the first item to be assembled in a piece of clothing. Because I needed to get the labels designed and woven, my back was up against the wall to develop something fast.

Thinking of a company name just to create a garment label was probably one of the poorest decisions I've ever made for a business, and the biggest mistake I made was that I added the word *clothing* to the brand name. That choice later came back to bite me in the butt when someone approached me wanting to do a custom perfume to partner with my apparel line, but it wasn't going to work with that inconvenient word *clothing* in the brand name.

Having learned my lesson from this major faux pas in naming my second company, I made it a point to give serious consideration to my subsequent company names. When I began to develop the product that would become my third company, it was six months before I finally decided upon the name. I probably spent three to four months working on a brand name for my fourth company before confirming it.

Brand Name Faux Pas

Here are just a few of the business name missteps I've encountered. Neither of these fashion brands is still in business, so I'll go ahead and share them here.

I once mentored a designer who was adding women's apparel to his menswear line. The designs involved a lot of braided pieces with a lot of wrapping around the body . . . kind of like a straightjacket. I will admit, the designs were pretty cool. But when the designer told me we wanted to call his brand For Insane Human, I had to keep a straight face while inside my mind was screaming, "Are you freaking kidding me?" I thought maybe *he* was insane.

I teamed up with his design mentor and we managed to convince him not to use the brand name For Insane Human. We advised him to use that name as his company name instead, and then create the fashion label under a different name. Fortunately he took our advice and ended up with the fashion label Bedlam, which was the location of England's first mental institution—a story he told on his hangtag to help make the connection for the consumer.

Another brand name boo-boo I advised against was The Naked Room. I thought this one was going to be a lingerie line, but I was wrong. It was supposed to be a women's apparel brand. Unfortunately this young lady just wasn't open to my advice that her brand name made no sense and that she was unlikely to attract consumers to her brand with that name.

Here are a few more entries on my *what were they thinking?* list:

- Smelly-No-More—this roll-on deodorant is sold in Asia.

- Collon—a Japanese brand of small tubular chocolate cookie with a chocolate filling. Really?

- Darkie Toothpaste—rebranded in 1989 and is now sold under the name of Darlie.

There is one more point I would like you to consider about brand names. Start-up entrepreneurs tend to default to using their own name or their initials as the name of the business, for example, Foster Taylor Consultancy or F&T Consultancy. Unless you are setting up a law firm or medical practice or you have a well-known reputation in your industry, I would avoid going down that road.

In general, people who will come to you are looking for products and services. They'll search online because they are looking for help, for solutions, for answers to their problem. That means they are typing their problem into the search box, and your new business is more likely to appear in their search results if your business name involves or indicates the problem you solve. F&T Consultancy on its own doesn't tell me how you can help me. Granted, you can add keyword phrases to be found in the metadata on the website backend, but if I were scrolling down a list of companies to help me with my problem, I'm not too sure I would stop on that kind of listing.

The same is true if someone were to pass me a business card with that name on it; it still doesn't tell me how you can help me. Now, if you added a few more words to it, like P&K Interior Design Consultancy, you're at least getting a bit closer to telling the world about the solution you offer.

Think toward the future. If one day your business was thriving and you wanted to sell it, how easy or difficult would it be? How practical would it be to sell the Peter Klein Consultancy once Peter has left the business? It may not be that easy for John Smith to come in and take over that business, with another person's name on it.

It may seem like I'm beating a dead horse here, but I can't do enough to stress the importance of having the right brand name for your business. Let's call that dead horse done and dusted and move on to the other elements to look at when creating your brand perception.

Brand Logos Help Create a Perception

Designing a logo for your brand can be as important as deciding on the name of your brand. The logo, as a visual element of your brand, contributes to the perception of your product or service. It also becomes one of your brand assets, so it's not something to be taken lightly.

It continues to amaze me when I see new entrepreneurs create a logo for the business they're developing before they've even decided on a business model. I think this stems from the excitement that comes with setting up a new business.

Entrepreneurs are so anxious to say, "Hey world, I'm in business!" that they rush into designing a logo they can slap on a business card.

Before getting into the nuts and bolts of creating a logo, you should at least know what purpose it will serve. Your logo is a visual representation of your brand identity that serves to convey the essence of your brand. It should be recognizable to the point that it can stand in to identify your product or service without your brand name being written out.

The logo aids in creating perception, so keep in mind how you want the client to feel about your brand. A logo can be an artistic design or symbol or it can simply be your brand name personified. Think Google, Subway, or Tiffany's, three examples of companies whose stylized name also doubles as a logo.

So, what should you consider when crafting that all important brand logo? Your logo should be simple, unique, memorable, and appropriate to your brand. The colors should also be in line with your corporate colors or if different, these alternative colors should at least make sense and tie in with the brand and its principal colors.

If you're considering having a design element for a logo, I strongly suggest that you hire a professional to work with you on this. And given that I feel you should leave logo design to the experts, I won't be going into the details of how to construct an amazing logo—that's just not my wheelhouse. There are a number of resources you can turn to for great logo design work at a reasonable price. You can find design freelancers on sites such as Fiverr, Upwork, and 99Designs.

Fiverr started out as a freelance marketplace where everything cost just $5. Today the starting price is usually more than that, but you can still find people offering services starting at a fiver. But remember—you get what you pay for. If you're just looking to test the waters, give more than one freelancer a crack at your logo for $5 or $10. An out-of-pocket expense of $15–30 to have three freelancers take on your project just might be the most efficient way to land yourself a fantastic-looking logo.

Using Upwork and 99Designs will cost significantly more. With Upwork you can set the dollar limit for your design and allow free-lancers to bid for the project. 99Designs, on the other hand, stipulates fixed fees for the various creative services their freelancers offer.

One last point you should consider when outsourcing creative works such as logo design or app development is that you never know if your brand is going to be the next big thing in your industry. *Can you tell that I'm an optimistic person?*

In this light, it would be wise to have the freelancer sign what's called a work-for-hire contract. This contract ensures that both you and the freelancer clearly understand the scope of project and what is expected of the freelancer. More importantly, this kind of contract specifies that you, as the person hiring the freelancer, have full legal rights to the artwork created on your behalf. This way when your business becomes the next big thing, they have no legal right to come back to claim royalties on the logo design.

Tap into the Senses

You know already that perception is created through the five senses of sight, sound, taste, touch, and smell. Thanks to information from their senses, customers will have a perceived idea about your brand before they buy anything from you.

Tapping into the senses can be a powerful way to motivate prospective consumers. Think of the cookie branding at work in a Famous Amos bakery, for example. Famous Amos taps into your sense of sight by visually displaying the goods in an attractive way. Baking on the premises ensures that your sense of smell will be actively engaged, and they encourage product sampling to bring your taste buds into play. Through careful brand management Famous Amos uses these sensory factors to create an emotional connection with the product, and that emotional connection, with all the anticipation involved, tends to lead to a purchase.

Maximize the Visual Elements

Most of us are visual creatures, so sense of sight is often the most significant one for you to work with when you're creating your brand.

The visual elements that you will tap into when creating your brand include your choice of brand colors (choose a primary and a secondary color), your choice of typeface or font, and your logo. Note that not every brand requires a logo.

Understanding color and its impact on perception is an essential step when deciding which colors to select. Your use of color is vital to creating a positive brand perception and powerful memory recall for prospects and consumers. The color you select should set you apart in the marketplace.

According to Satyendra Singh, people make up their minds within 90 seconds of their initial interactions with either people or products. About 62 to 90% of this assessment is based on colors alone. Prudent use of colors, then, can contribute not only to differentiating products from what competitors are offering, but also influences moods and feelings—positively or negatively—and therefore, people's attitude towards certain products.[35]

Tiffany has a strong brand perception. Ask any woman in the western world and she will likely recognize the iconic robin's-egg-blue gift box. The box alone is not the brand; it is, however, a powerful brand messenger. That distinctive blue box, which has become a Tiffany brand asset, immediately evokes thoughts of luxury, quality, and perhaps even being loved.

When I got married I appreciated all the generous gifts that we received; however, to be honest, I was most eager to open those boxes that were robin's-egg blue with white ribbon because I knew what was inside was going to be something special.

You can easily find information on the psychology of color and what each color represents as well as examples of brands and the color choices they've used to create their brand perception.

Typeface Tells a Story

What font or typeface to use? Though we often confuse the two terms, there is a difference between typeface and font. A typeface is the design of the letters and numbers, symbols, and other typographic elements that make up any given style. It's the actual shapes, curves and white space that make up the style of the characters and that let us put words on paper or screen.

A font, on the other hand, is the digital file you install on your computer and is traditionally defined as a complete character set within a typeface, often of a specific size and style. 12 pt. Gill Sans Bold and 10 pt. Gill Sans Italic are both fonts of the typeface Gill Sans.36

Nowadays you will see the words font and typeface used interchangeably. Since you are likely to speak to your graphic designer in terms of your choice of font, I will use that word for the purposes of this chapter.

The font you select will say a lot about your brand, so it's important for you to have an understanding of this key element in creating brand perception.

Most typefaces can be classified into one of four basic groups. The most common classifications are by technical style: serif, sans serif, script, and decorative.

Serifs are the little feet that the type sits on, and the little hooks that cap off a letter. Take a look at the font Times New Roman, for example, and notice the short lines at the top and bottom of each letter. They help your eye move from letter to letter.

Serif fonts tend to be used for magazines and newspapers as they provide a better user experience in print than they do on the web. Common serif fonts include Baskerville, Palatino, Georgia, Times New Roman, Bodoni, Garamond and Courier.

The word 'sans' means without, so the sans-serif typefaces are the ones without the feet or hooks. Because the letter is stripped down to its bare essence there is nothing to lead your eye to the next letter, making sans-serif fonts slightly harder to read.

San-serif type tends to be used for shorter messages such as titles, headlines and road signage. They tend to evoke an informal feel. San-serif fonts are best used onscreen, and they are a good choice for blogs or personal websites. Some of the most common sans-serif fonts are Arial, Helvetica, Verdana, Comic Sans, Gill Sans, Franklin Gothic, Lucida Sans, and Myriad Pro.

The fonts of the script group are cursive fonts. They tend to produce an elegant feel and are appropriate for headlines. Formal script fonts are derived from 17th-century formal writing styles. Many characters have elements that join them to other letters. Calligraphic script fonts mimic calligraphic writing and they can be connecting or non-connecting in design.

When you are unable to classify a font into any of the three general font styles I've just mentioned, then it most likely falls into the last category of decorative fonts. Most decorative fonts are custom creations and tend to be the most diverse in nature. They are rarely used for lengthy blocks of text and are more popular for signage.

Preview Your Company Name in Multiple Fonts

I hope you're seeing the importance of creating a perception about your brand and beginning to appreciate how you are solely responsible for developing this using color, font choice, and of course your business name. These elements are all linked together to create brand perception.

One very useful way to see how things are linked is to test them out in advance. Hop over to the website Dafont.com, where you will find a great tool that allows you to see what your brand name will look like in a variety of fonts—over 2580 of them at the time of this writing. Of course, you don't have to spend your time going through all those fonts; Dafont.com is set up to show you types of fonts grouped together, making it easy for you focus on the typefaces that are of interest to you.

Once you've decided on a font, you can upload it to your computer if you don't already have it on your system. From there you can start to play around with colors using that font.

I hope that you will give the development of your brand perception the time and effort it deserves. If you can grasp the importance of creating the ideal visual elements for your brand, which in turn establishes a perception in the mind of the target audience, you will be far ahead of the start-up entrepreneur who just picks a few colors and then hires a graphic designer to create a logo to slap on a website and business card.

Remember, the three elements that create brand perception are name, font, and color. This is where you get to have some fun and express your creativity, so take your time with this step of the process.

Jump onto the Start-up Action Step questions below to get the juices flowing and begin shaping your brand perception. If you're still up in the air as to what kind of product or service you want to offer, come back to this section when you are ready.

Start-up Action Steps

1. What is the brand perception you wish to create? What feelings or aspirations do you want associated with your product or service?

2. What company or product brand names would evoke the brand perception you outlined in the answer to the first question above? Keep in mind that this is something that you don't want to rush through. You can continue developing your business while sorting out the name.

3. What color will you consider to instill your desired brand perception? For example, primary colors are a good choice for children's brands and kindergartens.

4. What fonts will you use to shape your desired brand perception? You may want to establish your company name before choosing fonts.

5. What type of logo (should you have one) would create the desired brand perception?

Chapter 7

Positioning: Position Your Brand in the Mind of the Consumer

We spent a good deal of time discussing how to establish your brand perception so that the consumer sees you in a specific way and then gravitates to you. Our next topic, positioning, is the fifth element of the entrepreneurship path and has a lot in common with perception.

Ideally, the development of just the right name and the use of specific colors combined with the right font will create a perception of your brand that proclaims, "Hey world, this is what we are all about!" It's a kind of psychological manipulation, so to speak.

The process of brand positioning is similar. Simply put, it is the process of positioning your brand in your customer's mind and influencing what the consumer thinks and feels about your brand.

Take note, your brand will get positioned in prospective clients' minds even if you do not take an active role in developing your positioning. If you are proactive and take the time to think about this, you can positively influence your brand positioning in the eyes of your target market. If you don't, the consumer will determine your positioning—and it may not be what you had in mind.

In the previous chapter on perception I shared a quote from Al Ries and Jack Trout's fabulous *Positioning, the Battle for Your Mind*. I highly recommend that you get your hands on a copy of this book, as you begin tackling the topic of positioning. Here's what they say:

> *The basic approach of positioning is not to create something new and different, but to manipulate what is already in the mind, to retie the connections that already exist.*

—AL RIES AND JACK TROUT,
Positioning, the Battle for Your Mind[37]

As an entrepreneur building a new brand, it once again it falls onto your shoulders to establish how you want to be seen in the marketplace, and how to you want to position your brand in the minds of your prospects and customers.

Positioning is about creating an identity surrounding your brand, product, or service using pricing, distribution (where and how you sell your brand), packaging, and awareness of what the competition is doing.

The objective is to create a unique impression in the consumer's mind, an association that makes your brand distinctive in the marketplace, and so special and desirable that the consumer will think of your brand first, ranking it above that of any of your competitors.

As you begin brainstorming your positioning, consider how you may be able to carve out a special niche for yourself in the market. How can you create your own blue ocean strategy? If this notion is new to you, that's okay. The concept of the blue ocean strategy was developed, in the book of that name, by management consultants W. Chan Kim and Renée Mauborgne.

They noticed that companies within similar industries are likely to go head-to-head with one another to gain market shares. With more and more players fishing in the same ocean, or competing in the market, these companies fight over the same group of fish, or consumers, to the point they create a bloody red ocean.

Kim and Mauborgne believed that success would come to those companies who stopped competing in the red ocean and instead created their own blue oceans of untapped new markets offering growth potential, thereby making the competition irrelevant.

Designing your own blue ocean is one way to position yourself, to separate yourself from the competition and position yourself in the minds of your target audience so they think of your business when they need a solution to their problem.

You may feel, as a start-up entrepreneur, that your business is not big enough for you to be thinking about a blue ocean strategy. I think that is a limiting belief. I conduct my business as a small operation with the concept of a blue ocean strategy always in the back of my mind. You never know when an idea might pop into your head that can help you to stay two to three steps ahead of your competition.

Blue Ocean Strategy is worth reading, as it may help you when it comes time to sit down and brainstorm your thoughts and ideas on how to create that unique impression, which is your element of drama or mystique—what it is that you bring to the table that is unlike what's on offer by anyone else. This can be something so simple it might surprise even you.

For my kids' golf apparel business, for example, we added both a sun-protection and moisture-wicking treatment to the clothing to add that unique bit of something special to the brand's identity.

In this book's introduction I mentioned the women's clothing boutique I owned in the late '90s. There were plenty of other women's clothing stores in Singapore at the time, but what set us apart from most of the other retailers wasn't the fact that we offered unique resort wear. What made us different was one thing: sizing. Back then very few stores in town carried clothing that catered to the western-size body type (you know, full bosom and curvy hips and buttocks) or stocked sizes with two digits, 10, 12, 14—you get the idea. Catering to an underserved market was the primary reason for our success.

When we moved from the Chinatown area to the main city shopping area, we did another thing that repositioned us in the market: we changed what time we opened for business. At the time it was customary for retail stores not to open until 11:00 am and to close at 9:00 pm. With the shopping center sitting smack between two major hotels, there was always early morning traffic from tourists cruising the hallways to kill time, since they were unable to check into their rooms right away.

I saw this as an opportunity and switched our hours of operation so that we opened at 10:00 am and closed at 8:00 pm. This allowed us to better serve not only tourists from the hotels but also mothers with young kids at school, who seized the chance to get in early, shop, and be back home before the kids got off the school bus.

The boutique became positioned in the market as the go-to store to find affordable, comfortable, western-sized apparel with hours of operation that met consumers' needs.

Now it's time for you to brainstorm how you want to position yourself in your marketplace. What will set you apart from the other brands offering similar products or services? Is it possible for you to create your own blue ocean where you won't be in direct competition with those other brands?

Devising your positioning plan and your own blue ocean strategy will take some serious thought, so give yourself time and space for the creativity to kick in. You can begin with answering the questions in these Start-up Action Steps.

Start-up Action Steps

1. Think about where you feel your brand will likely be positioned in the market based on product, price, and location, or method of distribution.

2. Determine who are your direct competitors.

3. How are each of these competitors positioned? What makes them unique—or not?

4. Now that you've identified how your competitors are positioned, what makes you unique? Think about the element of mystique or drama that sets you apart.

5. Read *Positioning: The Battle for Your Mind,* by Jack Trout and Al Ries.

6. Visit the Blue Ocean case studies page (https://www.blueoceanstrategy.com/teaching-materials) and read about how Yellow Tail wines crafted a winning strategy in an overcrowded market.

Chapter 8

Pricing: Establishing Prices for Your Product or Service

Now that you've gained some clarity about positioning yourself in the marketplace, it's time to take the next step on the entrepreneur path: it's time to think about setting your product prices or establishing your consultation fees. Stick with me now, don't go running off just yet.

I can almost see the thought bubble over your head, "Should I really bother to read this chapter now when I don't even know what product or service I'm going to offer?" I understand where you're coming from, but I encourage you to explore this section anyway, as ideas or clarification about what type of product you want to offer may occur to you as you read about different options for pricing your goods and services.

Determining pricing can be a scary thought for a lot of people. When I created my first company, which was an apparel sourcing agency, the nature of the business meant that I was paid by commission on a per-unit basis for garments shipped to the client.

The factory quoted me a unit price for each style and as the middleman I simply added a fixed dollar amount on top of that and quoted the client the final FOB (freight on board) price. Once the goods shipped, I received my payment from the factory. It's a different world today and I could not sustain a living with today's low margins.

My second business, a ladies' fashion boutique, involved designing and manufacturing the clothes and hiring the staff to service the customers, plus running general day-to-day operations, so knowing about pricing became vital.

There are many books available that can take you in-depth on how to do pricing. For the sake of this chapter I'm simply going to cover the basics of pricing, because it would be impossible for me to go into detail about all the different types of business models.

Avoid This Major Pitfall

Before I get into specifics of how to set your prices, I do want to highlight a key mistake that many new business owners make that hurts them before they even open their doors for business. It's time we talked about a very crucial element to the success of your business—your mindset. Yes, I touched on the entrepreneur mindset in the first chapter, but this is a different thing, so please keep reading.

Many new business owners believe that because they are just starting out, they need to set their prices lower than the competition's prices. This is not true. Where did this notion come from? There is nothing carved into stone tablets that says, "Thou shalt start out with a disadvantage by lowering your prices, therefore making it harder for you to be successful."

If you were thinking this way, then stop it right now, and stop listening to anyone around you who tells you otherwise. It's normal to believe that because you're new, you haven't earned the right to charge market rates, but it's also bull-pucky.

Let's just bust the pricing myth right now. How you set your prices has a lot to do with your self-worth and how you value your own product and services. Pricing is the customer's measure of what he or she is willing to pay to receive the benefits associated with the purchase. Decide right now, from the start, that whatever it is that you offer the consumer, you will set your prices based on the brand perception you want to create and positioning strategy you've chosen. Most importantly, your prices will be based on the value of the transformation the consumer will gain from you, and not based on what people around you might be saying.

Determining a Selling Price

One of the most important aspects of establishing your business is determining your pricing in a way that allows you to maximize profits. When your product is priced properly you will see better sales.

The price you set for your product or service is based not only on the cost of making and marketing the product, but also on your desired margin of profit. Ultimately, your price is also based on what the market will bear.

As an entrepreneur, it's important that you look at the big picture when setting your fees or product price. One mistake that many newbie entrepreneurs make when setting prices is that they look solely at the item to be priced. Often small business owners fail to consider the value of their own labor, their time, and the effort that goes into business operations and getting that product to market. This leads them to undervaluing the product when they set the price. I am pointing this out here and now to help you avoid making this big mistake.

Depending on the product or service, the dilemma you face is whether to aim for an increase in volume with lower prices or a high price that yields a lower volume. Before you go and pull a price randomly from the air, you'll need to do a bit of research and planning. This is not something to be taken lightly, as it could easily make you or break your business.

There is no one-size-fits-all formula for pricing products and services for every business. Only you will be able to determine what is right for you. My role here is to outline the factors you will want to consider when determining your fee or product price.

As you begin to look at the following key factors to address, I want you to recall the brand perception you want to achieve. Also, think about how you envision positioning your brand in the market. Both of these elements will influence the price that you will set.

If your brand perception is that of a high-end product or service, then it makes sense to reflect this with a higher price. If you plan to position yourself as a high-end brand within a luxury office location, consumers will naturally expect the price to reflect that.

The following are a few key factors you'll want to consider when establishing the ideal price for your product or service.

Know Your Market

The second element of the entrepreneur path, if you'll recall, is *person*, or target market. You've already done a deep dive into who this person is, to understand their lifestyle, financial status, and other factors that might give you a general idea of their discretionary income.

Armed with the information you have about your ideal client, you are in a better position to determine what price range will work best for them, or more importantly, how high you can set your price without creating resistance in your ideal client.

Determine the True Cost of the Product

It is imperative that you know the true cost of your product. When I say true cost, I mean everything that went into developing a physical product, from sampling to employing graphic designers or freelancers, to courier costs, to brochures, etc. It's key that you also include the cost of your own labor.

To calculate your personal hourly rate, take the amount of money you wish to earn per year (remember to make this a personal salary, not business profits) and divide that by 2000 (the number of working hours in a year based on a 40-hour work week). The resulting number will be your hourly rate.

Now take your hourly rate, times the number of hours you worked on a product, consultation package, or service structure, and add that to the cost of the product to get to your true cost. Newbie entrepreneurs tend to disregard the time and effort spent on product or service development and leave their own compensation out of the cost of goods.

Know Your Monthly Overheads

Given that so many people work from home these days, thinking about monthly operational overheads is not obvious, and many start-up entrepreneurs skip this important consideration.

Even when you are working from home, you're still going to be using basic utilities such as electricity and water and office space within the house (even if it is your spare bedroom or the dining room table). Check with your state or country tax department to see what tax exemptions you can get for these items. In the meantime, you should still be looking at these factors as expenses that need to be accounted for in your overall pricing.

Here's a caveat about including overheads based on a home office. I want you to start thinking long-term. You might be comfortable working from your home office now; however, in the future you may wish to move into a serviced office or a co-working space. The monthly expense of an outside office is likely be significantly higher than your home office overheads.

I suggest that you estimate the price the future cost of an office and build that rate into your overall cost of goods, rather than the home-office rate. This way when you're ready to make a move you don't have to make sizeable leaps in fees or prices to cover the cost, because you've taken this expense into account from the start.

Now that you've determined your overhead cost, add that to the product cost of goods. This figure becomes the true cost of goods.

Understand the Customer's Perceived Value

The value your customer perceives is based on the product itself plus intangibles such as service, quality, and specialized expertise. Perceived value is also about how the consumer values the results, the benefits, or the transformation that he or she will gain.

If the consumer views the results your product or service produces as average, the perceived value is average. If, on the other hand, they can see how life is going to be significantly better—if their perception is that they will make money, save money, save time, avoid loss, gain pleasure, gain popularity, or be more comfortable thanks to your product or service, then the perceived value is higher and a higher price is warranted.

Know Your Competition

Your competition is something that you considered when you did your competitive analysis as part of the action steps at the end of the chapter on positioning.

Knowing how your competitors are perceived and priced in the marketplace will give you great insights on how to determine your own pricing. Again, I want to caution you against significantly lowering your price with the aim of making a competitive entrance in your market. This strategy often backfires and you end up pricing yourself out of business. Instead, raise your price and give more value. What that looks like will be determined by you and your industry.

The way you add value need not be something expensive. It can be something as simple as an automated, content-rich monthly newsletter that can be sent out to your clients or even to their clients. Another possibility is a free 20- to 30-minute follow-up call 30 to 45 days after service to see how the client is getting on with the product. You'll brainstorm ideas for a value-add later, in your Start-up Action Steps for this chapter.

Calculate Your Break-even Point

To be profitable in your business you must identify your break-even point, or the point at which total revenue equals total costs or expenses. There is no profit or loss at this point—you're just breaking even.

The break-even point is an important measurement in understanding the health of an established company. However, it's just as useful a tool for the newbie entrepreneur because it allows you to tweak things before you open your doors for business.

Knowing your break-even point is helpful in deciding prices, setting sales budgets, and preparing a business and marketing plan. Think of the break-even calculation as a tool that will allow you to analyse the critical profit drivers of your business such as sales volume, your production costs, and your average sales price.

To determine your break-even costs, take your most current income statement and identify expense items as either fixed costs or variables. Fixed costs or expenses include salaries, payroll taxes, benefits, rent, utilities, insurance, accounting, and interest. Fixed costs are independent of sales. Variable expenses include things like the cost of goods, commissions, travel, and freight, and these expenses rise and fall with sales.

Use the following formula to calculate the break-even cost.

BE: fixed costs ÷ (price − variable cost) = break-even point in units sold

The breakeven point is equal to the total fixed costs divided by the difference between the unit price and variable costs. Note that in this formula, fixed costs are stated as a total of all overheads for the business, whereas price and variable costs are stated as per-unit costs— the price for each product unit sold.

Let's look at the example below and assume your business is Imperial Enterprises.

Imperial Enterprises has calculated that it has fixed costs that consist of its lease, the depreciation of its assets, its executive salaries, and its property taxes. Those fixed costs add up to $65,000. Their product is the widget. Their variable costs associated with producing the widget are raw material, factory labor, and sales commissions. Variable costs have been calculated to be $0.85 per unit. The widget is priced at $2.10 each.

Given this information and using the formula above, we can calculate the break-even point for the Imperial Enterprises widget:

$$\$65,000 \div (\$2.10 - \$0.85) = 52,000 \; units$$

Based on the fixed costs, selling price, and variable costs, Imperial Enterprises has to sell 52,000 units to break even before profit. As we have no idea of the demand for the widget, it could take a while before this company hits its break-even point.

I'm a believer in reaching profitability sooner than later. As a start-up entrepreneur you can look at the different variables in the formula and then determine where you might be able to make adjustments to help you to arrive at and surpass your break-even point sooner.

When reviewing the fixed costs for a bricks-and-mortar operation like Imperial Enterprises, you might opt for a different location with lower rent. You may also choose to reduce starting salaries from what you'd planned to reduce the overall fixed costs. Your new fixed costs dropped to $58,000.

Both the retail price and the variable costs could also be adjusted. The retail price might increase slightly, by 20 to 30 cents, and perhaps you managed to get the cost of fabricating the widget down to $0.80 per unit.

Plugging in our new numbers, we now get the following:

$$\$58,000 \div (\$2.40 - \$0.80) = 36,250 \; units$$

That's a heck of a lot better than 52,000 units. Even if we keep the original fixed costs untouched and only adjust the purchase price and the cost of goods, we are still able to significantly reduce the number of units it would take to break even.

$65,000 ÷ ($2.40 - $0.80) = 40,625 units

This is the beauty of running a break-even calculation before you open your doors for business, when it's a lot easier to make the kinds of changes we discussed above.

Keep in mind that you are not profitable until you have sold at least one unit over the break-even number, so you'll want to get to this point as quickly as you can.

This is one reason working from home and significantly lowering overhead remains an attractive option for the start-up entrepreneur.

Pricing Strategies

Now that you've read about some of the pitfalls to avoid and the areas to research before you set your price, you're ready to look at a few different pricing strategies.

For entrepreneurs, price determination is often a function of the cost of production and the desired level of markup.

Suggested or Going Rate

In suggested-rate or going-rate pricing, the product is priced according to the rates prevailing in the market—that is, on par with competitors' prices, though you may sometimes charge more or less depending on market conditions.

With the going-rate pricing method, business owners feel secure that their prices will make them as attractive as any of their competitors to potential customers.

Full-Cost-Plus Pricing (Markup Method)

Full-cost-plus pricing is a price-setting method in which you add together the direct material cost, direct labor cost, selling cost, and overhead cost of the product, then add that sum to a markup percentage to come up with the price of the product.

Notice I've included the direct labor cost in this calculation. Remember, just because you work from home or you don't have staff working for you, it doesn't mean that you should forego adding in the cost of your own labor. Many start-up entrepreneurs make the big mistake of not including the cost of their time and operational overheads in the equation because they aren't drawing a salary—so no direct labor cost—or because they work from home—so overhead is "free."

Helloo . . . you are paying for this. Whether it's you or someone else paying the bill, it costs money to keep those lights and radiators on, or to run that air conditioner. Find out what you are legally allowed to claim for tax allowances and use that amount to determine your monthly overheads.

Even if you aren't going to immediately draw a salary—which is another no-no, you should pay yourself first—it's important that you allow for the cost of salary (or salaries) and overheads to be included in the pricing from the onset. This way they're built into the price and you're covered for later on down the road.

Gross Margin Pricing

Gross margin pricing is a pricing method where markup percentage is based on the product's total production cost.

Gross margin, also known as gross profit, is the selling price minus the wholesale or direct costs of your product or service. When expressed in percentage terms, gross margin represents profit as a percentage of revenues (excluding indirect costs like rent or other overheads).

To determine gross margin, you will take the difference between 1) the cost to produce or purchase an item, and 2) its selling price. If it cost a company $28 to produce a product that then sells for $40, the product's gross margin is $12 (40 − 28 = 12), or 30% of the selling price (12 ÷ 40 = 30).

Gross margin pricing might work well for small business owners, manufacturers, distributors and retailers who sell a small number of products to a limited clientele, and whose overhead costs are relatively small and totally unrelated to the products sold or customers served.

Markup Method

In the markup pricing method, the seller calculates the cost of purchasing or producing the product and then adds a desired markup to it. Markup pricing uses product costs and percentage markups to calculate the selling price of a product. It ignores operating expenses (marketing and administration expenses).

This pricing strategy is often used by business owners who acquire products from suppliers and then uses a percentage increase on top of the product cost to arrive at their final price.

Let's say, for example, that you have a lighting store. You have a floor lamp that cost $450 plus $50 for shipping and handling; therefore it costs you $500 per lamp you purchase and have shipped to your business. Using the markup pricing method, you determine your desired or ideal gross margin and you mark up the price accordingly.

If you were to mark up the price by 50% of the total cost, then you'll make $250 from the sale of each floor lamp (50% x $500 = $250). Your selling price on each floor lamp, then, would be $750 ($500 cost + $250 markup).

Our lighting-store example deals with a markup based on cost of goods plus shipping, yet many small business owners like to translate markups on cost into what is known as markup based on selling price.

To calculate a markup based on selling price, you divide the planned dollar markup on the product by the planned selling price. Using our example above, we would do the calculation as follows:

Markup % on selling price = Dollar Markup ÷ Selling Price

Markup % on selling price = $250 ÷ $750 = 33.3%

Thus the markup cost is 50% and the markup on selling price is 33.3%. Although the percentages are different, the profit made on the floor lamp remains the same at $250.

The markup method is pretty straightforward and simple and allows you to set your prices rather quickly. Just keep in mind that using this method of pricing, you are not considering any overhead expenses of the business.

Keystone Pricing

Keystone is a retail term for a pricing method of marking your merchandise for resale to an amount that is double the wholesale price, or cost, of the merchandise. In a nutshell, keystone pricing means that if the wholesale price of the product is $40, then the price for the consumer would be set at $80. This is a 50%initial markup (IMU).

Keystone pricing reflects two levels of markup. The first is from the vendor or manufacturer to the retailer, and the second is from the retailer to the customer. If we look at the example just given, the vendor paid $20 to make the product and then sold it for $40 to the retailer, who sold it to the customer for $80. Traditional retail sales have predominantly followed this markup model.

When I worked with fashion apparel brands, most started their pricing at keystone, in other words, doubling the cost from the vendor and then increasing it from there. The keystone price was essentially their baseline.

To effectively mark up your products, consider what others within your industry are doing. Customers today can easily search online to compare prices so you'll want to check out the going rates. Depending on your industry, you too can search online to determine going rates and use them as a point of reference.

Not every new entrepreneur will be selling products. You may decide to offer your services as a consultant, and the advanced research that will help you set your consulting fees is similar to what you do for pricing products. Let's look at consulting fees now.

How to Set your Consulting Fee

In *The Consulting Bible, Everything You Need to Create and Expand a Seven-Figure Consulting Practice*, Alan Weiss teaches us that "value trumps fee."[38] I love that.

Fees are based on value, and it will be your role to demonstrate your value before you even get into a discussion about fees. You have a few options when it comes to determining how you will bill for your services.

When it comes to determining fee structure you can price by the hour, by the day, by project, or on a retainer basis. Most entrepreneurs who are transitioning into consulting will use either a daily rate or an hourly rate. This can be a good option when first starting out and when you have yet to determine what your client will want.

Another option is a project-based rate. This method of pricing requires you to know the details of the project, as well as your personal time requirements to get the project done. If you don't need to bring other vendors into the project, this method could be a good option.

The downside to the method comes into play when a project gets delayed by the client or you are asked to make significant changes to the project. Experiencing a delay or being asked to redo aspects of the project can result in a lower hourly rate when averaged over the course of the project. You also need to beware of scope creep, also known as requirement creep, where a project involves continuous or uncontrolled requirements outside of what was originally negotiated for. Scope creep can occur when the details and requirement of the project are not clearly defined at the onset of the project. You may wish to consider adding a small buffer into your fee to allow for these kinds of delays and/or cover the additional cost of your time. And when a client asks for more than what was contracted for, be willing to say, "This is beyond the scope of the project."

Consultants who work on retainer basis sign a retainer agreement with the client. This structure is ideal for you as a consultant, as it allows you to have money upfront.

To use the retainer method you will decide an hourly rate and the number of hours the project will take. You then ask your client to pay in advance. The advantage of being paid in advance is that it guards against potential non-payment by the client.

If this is how you chose to set up your business model, it is important that you focus on building long-term relationships with the individuals and companies you work with rather than investing time in a string of one-off clients.

Your Business Will Determine the Fee or Product Price

The price you set for your product or service will have a direct influence on your marketing strategy. I will be covering marketing in an upcoming chapter. In the meantime, as you've gone through this chapter on pricing strategies and consulting fees, perhaps one or two methods have jumped out at you. With that in mind, you should be able to get started on the questions below in your Start-up Action Steps.

Ready, set, go!

Start-up Action Steps

1. Calculate your overheads and product or service expenses to determine your true cost.

2. Review how your competitors' products or services are priced in the market. What are their pricing strategies?

3. Do your customers expect a certain price range?

4. Establish your market share goals. In other words, what percent of the total sales within your industry would you like your company to achieve?

5. Determine how your pricing will affect your sales volume goals.

6. Determine how your method of distribution (in-store, on-line, face-to-face, or wholesale) will affect your price.

7. Decide which price-setting method you will use. Is your goal to sell at a higher price, at a lower price, or at the same as your competitor? Why?

8. How does the nature of your product or service affect the price? For example, if you are a florist you may increase prices over holiday periods to account for changes in supply and demand, and if you are an accountant you might charge more for rush jobs during tax season.

9. Run the numbers to determine your break-even point. Then explore where you can make adjustments to overheads or reductions in the product/service cost and subsequent price. Such adjustments will reduce your break-even point to achieve and increase profits.

10. What type of value-add can you offer the client without a significant increase in your own investment in terms of time, delivery, or development? [Note: Automated newsletters and audios make for great value-adds.]

Chapter 9

Place of Distribution: Where and How Will you Distribute Your Product or Service?

If you've ever taken some form of entrepreneurship or marketing course, you are bound to have heard or read about the Four Ps of Marketing. If you're familiar with this concept, think of this discussion as a quick refresher. If this term is new to you, the Four Ps are *product, place, price and promotion,* otherwise known as the marketing mix.

You'll notice that the concept of *place* figures both among the Four Ps and in the steps of our Entrepreneurship Path Framework. You might naturally assume that *place* refers to the location where you go to buy products and services—the mall, the grocery store, a car dealership—or the bricks and mortar locations where the consumer comes to you, or the place of business where you conduct your service-based business.

It makes sense to think this way, but as a business owner you need to be thinking differently. When you begin to explore how to develop your products and services, you must also begin to consider how your goods will be made available for purchase to the public.

Today you have so many options. You can sell your goods from your own retail store, sell goods wholesale, sell to a distributor, sell online, sell over the phone, or even through home parties.

Nowadays, how and where—the *place* where you sell your goods and services—has expanded greatly, giving buyers and sellers more opportunities to do business. The beauty is that business owners are no longer pigeonholed into having just one way to sell their wares. That's good news, as it offers you multiple streams of revenue.

This is a key issue to be thinking about—how many ways can you offer your solution(s) to the consumer, be it a product or service, and how many different price points would meet consumers' needs? Let me give you an example of what this might look like.

Let's use the example of Susie Smith, who is selling candles made with organic beeswax. Susie designs and buys the candles directly from the manufacturer. She has several options for distributing, or placing, her candles.

She can sell the candles at a wholesale price to a retail chain, which will then sell the candles to their customers at their desired price. Susie is more likely to sell more than one piece, as goods are sold in bulk, and to multiple retail stores. The selling price might be her cost plus a small amount for profit; however, she is likely to sell in high enough volume to still make a profit.

Susie maintains her own website, which allows her to make retail sales directly to consumers, and perhaps at a lower price than the price at which the above-mentioned retailer would sell her candles. The cost of shipping is at the expense of the customer, so her profit margin can be significantly higher than if she were selling wholesale.

Another option for Susie could be selling directly to consumers at home parties. Granted this involves of the minor hassle of having to bring the product to the home of the party host; however, she can still charge a price that might be the same or slightly lower than the price on her website. Or it may be the same as online, and the host gets either a commission fee or product in exchange for hosting the party.

In Susie's neighbourhood there is a small gift shop whose owner loves her candles and with whom she has a consignment arrangement. When candles are sold, Susie gets a percentage of the sale price.

That percentage amount was negotiated between the owner and Susie when they agreed on the arrangement, and the shop owner doesn't purchase goods in advance—Susie only makes money when there is a sale. In the event the merchandise doesn't sell, the candles will be returned to her.

The last option Susie might have for distributing her goods would be in her own store. Given the monthly overheads she incurs, the price of candles sold in her store might be slightly higher than sold anywhere else.

As you can see, there are multiple ways to place your products in front of consumers, and at different price structures and with different profit margins.

Let's look at *place* from the viewpoint of a consultant. We'll say Bob Johnson is a marketing consultant, and he too has a few choices of how to sell or distribute his services.

Bob can work directly with clients at their place of business, offering his services face-to-face. Given the personalized nature of his service, the fee for consultation at the client's office is likely to be at the high end of what Bob charges.

If the consultation takes place remotely via video conferencing, Bob can still offer his consultation services face-to-face, and for what may or may not be the same fee charged when going to an office. Bob might offer clients a lower consultation fee if he is able to converse with them, using technology, from the comfort of his own office.

Another way Bob distributes and sells his knowledge is as a paid keynote speaker at conferences or business summits. He may also be a paid to speak at a lunch-and-learn session or a breakfast briefing.

The other method Bob uses to reach a much wider audience is to sell his knowledge through the online modular courses that he has developed. The beauty of the online courses is that Bob can still help a lot of people without having to personally deliver the information, as it is drip-fed to the consumer's inbox.

Whether you are selling a physical product or consulting services, your goal at this stage is to identify the different ways that consumers can buy from you. Not everyone can or wants to buy the top-of-the line product, so figure out how you can give them what they want at different price points.

Review these Start-up Action Steps to put your thoughts down on paper.

Start-up Action Steps

1. When we talk about *place* we're referring to the method of distribution you choose for your product or service. What are the different ways you can offer your product, service, solution, or system to the consumer?

2. Will you sell one piece at a time or in bulk?

3. Will you wholesale, direct sell face-to-face, retail at a bricks-and-mortar store, sell online, or offer products on consignment?

4. What are the different price points at which you can sell your product or service?

5. What are the different online platforms or places where you can retail your product or service?

6. List out as many external factors as you can that you need to consider as part of your distribution such as shipping, consignment contracts, commissions, taxes, affiliate fees, commute time, and cost.

7. Review and calculate the profit margins of your different methods of distribution.

Chapter 10

Platform: Showcasing and Promoting Your Product or Service

We've arrived at the last element of the entrepreneurship path, *platform*, which is my favourite of them all to work on. Basically, *platform* is the way you will showcase your business; it is all about how you will promote your brand and get the word out to the marketplace about what you offer—in other words, how you help.

Marketing is about creating an effective message and delivering it to the right audience at the right place and at the right time. That means you need to ensure that you are speaking to the right people (your target audience—the people who are experiencing a pain, problem, want, or need that you've already identified); that you're reaching them where they hang out, either online or offline, where they are watching TV, or in the magazines or trade publications they are reading; and that you're catching them at the right time (when they are paying attention to or consuming any of the above-mentioned forms of media).

Marketing is such an important element and ongoing process that I'll be spending a significant amount of time in this area. My years of working with small business owners and small and mid-sized enterprises have shown me that when it comes to marketing a business, it is the process of establishing a marketing strategy that causes the most confusion.

I'm always amazed by the number of people who, when asked who they sell to, say, "Everyone." *Wrong!* No, you don't! When you try to be everything to everyone, you're nothing to no one. Not everyone is your customer.

Once a participant at a talk I was giving insisted that everyone was his customer. He sold a peanut-based snack product, and when I challenged him about the customers who would not buy his product, because of a peanut allergy or because they simply didn't like peanuts, he replied, "Well, those people, they don't count. I sell to everyone else." He totally missed the point, and he wasn't open to the fact that not everyone would buy his product.

In this chapter you're going to learn about a variety of marketing tactics, or methods for reaching and engaging potential customers, that you can use for your business to create awareness and help you generate leads.

Before getting into the tactics, there are three things that you must first consider at the start of any marketing campaign: your marketing objective or goal, your budget for the campaign or project, and the timeline for the campaign.

Marketing Objectives

Far too often I've seen employees of small companies thrown into a marketing role and then told to make it rain with leads and new business. These individuals are given the title of "marketing manager," or the like, and while they may have some knowledge of tactics, they jump in without a plan.

Before deciding on any marketing tactics, you must first determine the objective or the goal of the campaign. You need to ask yourself what it is that you are trying to achieve. Is your goal to create awareness for the brand, to inform the public of a new product or service, or to drive traffic to a website or physical location? Or is the aim of your campaign to boost sales? Once this goal has been set, you need to look at the budget.

Marketing Budget

After you've identified your marketing objectives you're still not ready to dive into the tactics. The next step is to set a budget for the marketing campaign, a budget tailored to meet your objective or goal. You might want to consider having a monthly marketing budget or an annual budget that you draw from when you have a project that you want to promote.

The extent of the funds that get set aside for each of your marketing campaigns will determine that campaign's length. The budget will also determine which tactics you can utilize for your campaign. Naturally, the more money you have, the more options you have.

Regardless of the budget, I always start with guerrilla marketing tactics first (the free and low-cost strategies). After that I look at tactics that will incur an expense and take it from there.

Marketing Timeline

Okay, you're almost ready for the fun of putting together your marketing campaign. You've decided on a goal and set the budget, and now you need to set the timeline for the campaign and determine how long it will run. Will it be one week, two weeks, a month, or more? Campaign length is a key element to consider because it impacts the campaign budget—and vice versa.

For extended timelines you're going to need a bigger budget to allow you to employ a variety of tactics. But there's another way to look at it: with a fixed budget the longer the timeline, the less money you may have to spend altogether, and therefore the fewer paid tactics you need to employ.

Avoid the Marketing Campaign Dilemma – Prepare a Marketing Calendar

It can be a serious issue when you want to create a campaign but you don't have an adequate budget for it because you've used up the annual budget in the first two quarters of the year. Avoid that headache from the start by creating a marketing calendar, in October, for the following year.

If you're coming to the end of the year, then sit down with a calendar for the following year. If you're just getting started, then by all means do this exercise now. With a monthly calendar in front of you, go through each month and look at the local, national, and international events that take place during that month. Think about whether the event is something that you can tap into for promoting your business.

Determine if it is worthwhile to create some type of marketing campaign around this event. If so, make a note of this in the calendar. Do this for each month of the calendar year. Now go back and see if there are any events that are specific to your industry that you can take advantage of. If so, mark those down as well. For the following year you may wish to create an event to celebrate your business anniversary.

With the dates in the calendar, now go back and brainstorm on the various events you've identified. Decide on the objective that you want to achieve for each event or holiday, then set a budget and a timeline. Once you've done this, work backward to determine the dates when you must start working on individual marketing campaigns in order to meet your launch-date goals.

To recap, you will start with the objective for your campaign, allocate a budget, and set the timeline for running the campaign. Now it's time to jump into the marketing tactics you'll use.

Let the fun begin.

Marketing Tactics

With information so easily accessible on the web, today's consumer has often done their homework about your company before the conversation even begins, if what you're offering interests them. In this digital age the role of marketing is to provide educational information in an engaging way (infotainment marketing) that will bring consumers to your website or blog, where you can then capture their details (name and email address) to continue the conversation with them after they've left your site.

A marketing tactic is nothing more than a way for us to get the attention of our ideal customer or prospect. Marketing tactics that connect us to a prospect are also referred to as touchpoints. Gone are the days when four touchpoints were enough to get the prospect to go out to buy your product. Today it's more like 12 to 14 touchpoints. Yikes!

The reason for this in increase in consumer touchpoints is that people are bombarded with so many marketing messages every day—in their inbox, with online banner advertising, Facebook feed ads, billboards, TV commercials (if they even watch them), mobile ads, newspaper ads, and direct mail pieces—that the brain eventually begins to drown them out. As the marketer for your brand, you'll have to do more, or at the very least do something different, to rise above the noise.

Marketing tactics as a stand-alone activity do not work. The goal is to look at the different tactics together with the budget to create a cohesive strategy. Put another way, when I say you are working on a marketing strategy, it means that you are working on a marketing campaign.

Granted, you will need to create multiple touchpoints with prospects. However, pulling together different tactics is why I find marketing enjoyable. I like having the freedom to think outside the box and create multichannel campaigns (where each touchpoint is viewed as a channel, or a path to reach the consumer) that are fun, interesting, and educational for my prospects.

Another reason for multichannel marketing takes us back to the definition of the marketing process. Marketing means getting the message out to the right audience at the right place and time. Sometimes certain tactics work best in a certain place or at a certain time, so bear that in mind when you sit down to map out your campaign strategies.

Know that there are 101 ways to wash the dishes, and there are just as many ways that you can get out in front of your target audience. Don't let anyone tell you that their way is the only way to market *your* business, as that is simply horse manure.

Given that there are so many things that you could be doing, pick and choose tactics that are easy for you to execute, and that you can execute consistently without a huge financial expense. As your business grows, you'll be able to spend more.

Quite frankly, even as my business grows, I like to practice guerrilla marketing, or those tactics that are either low cost or even better, free. As a 50–60 Something Start-up Entrepreneur, you'll find that managing or stretching your resources will be key for the first few years.

All right, let's dive into some of the different tactics. To make things a bit easier I've grouped them by word-of-mouth, offline, and online tactics.

Word-of-Mouth Marketing Tactics

Word-of-mouth tactics are self-explanatory; however, for the sake of clarity, this tactic means simply getting out and speaking to people face-to-face about your business, whether in groups or one-on-one.

Listed below are a few of the ways you can seek out opportunities to introduce others to your business.

Business Networking Events

Attending regular networking events is a great way to be seen and to introduce yourself and your brand to other people. Create an introduction, a soundbite as it were, that tells people who you are, what your company is called, and the transformation your business provides. Notice that I used the word transformation.

If we go back to the chapter about product, you may recall learning that people don't buy products and services; they buy the results or the transformation that they believe they will gain or experience once they've made a purchase.

Network with the intention of introducing your brand to at least five new people. Don't fall into the trap of just hanging out with the people that you came with or that you know already. Say hello, exchange the basic pleasantries, and then move on if it turns out that your conversation partner is not a good fit for you. You're there to get leads for your business. Save the discovery session, or in-depth conversation with a prospect to learn more about them and their needs, for a coffee meeting or a phone call.

Face-to-Face Meetings

Some would argue that a face-to-face meeting would be considered a sales call, but we can look at it as a marketing tactic too. It's always a good thing if you can set a face-to-face meeting as it allows you to learn about the prospect's pain and problems and then offer the solution you provide to take away that pain.

Discover what it is that the prospect needs and avoid offering them your full buffet of products or services. Build a relationship first, and sell one thing at a time. Later, once you've built rapport and trust, you can offer the next solution.

It's likely that you will be doing a lot of face-to-face meetings at the outset of your business, as you get out to do the meet-and-greet routine, and your objective is to seek out new business. Time is money so ensure that you're making the most of your meetings. Come prepared with an objective and some literature that the prospect can take home with them and limit the meeting to about 45 minutes to an hour.

Speaking

Stop. Don't say it! If you are one of those people who say they would rather die than speak in front of a group of people, let me stop you before you put that out there and begin to sabotage yourself.

I'm not saying that you must get in front of an audience of 300 or more people—though an insightful entrepreneur would recognize that as a major opportunity to reach over 300 people who have already been pre-qualified as your target audience.

What I am suggesting is that you find opportunities to put yourself in front of smaller groups of people and offer to speak at events like Chamber of Commerce meetings, Rotary Clubs, and other industry-related associations.

Sometimes you will be asked not to "sell from the stage," however there are ways to seed your talk. Seeding is a tactful technique for generating sales by dropping into the conversation a casual mention of something that you offer. The aim of seeding is to pique the interest and curiosity of the audience with information that will have people seeking you out after the presentation.

Even if you're not there to sell explicitly, the advantage of speaking in front of groups is that it positions you as an industry expert. You want to be viewed as the go-to guy or gal in your field.

Another benefit of speaking at events is that when you have a great message and you're educating people in the industry, you may be invited as a guest speaker to address a larger audience. These could be free or paid engagements. If you become good at this, speaking can become an additional source of revenue for you.

Networking, face-to-face meetings, and speaking involve something you do every day—talking. Don't get bogged down in the mechanics, just be yourself and have a conversation. When you know that your role is to be of service to people or companies that really need your help, talking about your solution will become second nature.

Offline Marketing Tactics

Just as the term implies, offline marketing tactics are those activities which are not related to any web use. Offline tactics are varied, to say the least. I'll cover some tactics you are likely to want to use for your own business at some point in time.

Let's start with one thing that every start-up entrepreneur should have when launching a new business—a stationary suite.

Create an Engaging Stationary Suite

Earlier in this book we spent an entire chapter discussing perception. There I covered the importance of developing your brand name, colors, and fonts. Getting your stationary suite right can have a huge impact on your ability to gain new business, as it is the first impression people may have about you.

For my first company, I spent good money to have my stationary suite designed and printed on quality stock paper. Everything about it was high end, I'd even say regal, with a gold embossed logo.

Keep in mind that this is before email was a big thing and so my means for reaching out to prospective companies was via the post, using letting my stationary represent me. I also had a folder of readymade documents that allowed me to create press kits to pass out to buyers when I attended trade shows.

Although I was a one-person operation, most people who received my letters or press kids thought I worked for a large company—and that was exactly the impression that I wanted them to have.

Your stationary suite consists of your branded letterhead, envelope, business card, thank-you card, and maybe a branded folder. You might even want to consider including a *with compliments* slip.

A *with compliments* slip is simply a piece of paper, designed in your brand theme, which contains the same contact information as your letterhead or business card. This piece of paper features the words *with compliments* followed by your hand-written note.

For my current business I do not have a *with compliments* slip; instead I have two A5 folded cards that are branded with the company logo on the back. On the front of one of the cards it says *Thank You* and the front of the other card is blank. I use the blank card in place of a *with compliments* slip.

The most important element of your stationary suite is your business card. That small piece of card stock speaks volumes, so don't waste this precious marketing opportunity to promote yourself and your business. The business card should give your name, company name, and your job title. Your title is your designation, or your role in your business or company, and the form it takes will depend on customs in the country where you live. Some people choose to forgo a title on their business card, as a matter of personal choice, but keep in mind that an appropriate title can help to establish credibility.

When adding your phone contact details include your area code, and if your business deals with international customers, include your country code preceded by a + sign. Some people don't have any experience dialling internationally, so make it easy for them to reach you.

The actual design of your card will be up to you and your designer. However, here are a few things you should consider when creating your card.

- ➢ Use a professional design service, not your next door neighbor's grandkid.

- ➢ Use a quality card stock—use either 14-point cardstock (thick) or 16-point (thicker).

- ➢ The font size should be a minimum of 3 mm in height, or 10–11 points for the body and 7–8 for the contact information.

- ➢ Be sure to include your USP (your unique selling proposition, or what you do—this can be demonstrated as a tag line or itemized on the back of your card).

In addition to the stationary suite, three similar items that fall into the offline category are brochures, greeting cards, and postcards.

A brochure is not a must, particularly a printed brochure. A brochure in a digital format can be an important tool as part of your marketing arsenal; the advantage of a printed brochure (or even a double-sided document) is that it allows you to leave something behind with a prospect after a meeting has concluded.

Postcards and greeting cards are often overlooked as an effective marketing tactic. They both fall under the category of direct mail pieces; items sent out directly to a prospect or consumers' home address or place of business with *their name* on it, not addressed to the "current resident."

There are many business owners, who won't use direct mail because they feel it is expensive. During the late 90s when email was not what it is today, we relied heavily on direct mail—mainly postcards—to reach our retail customers.

Granted, it is easier and cheaper today to reach consumers in their email inbox, yet as a business owner you are now competing with everyone else vying to get inbox attention.

I take the opposite approach and send greeting cards and thank-you cards. I start preparing my holiday greeting cards in October. I do two covers, one that has a Christmas theme and one that is more generic for my non-Christian clients. The back is branded with the company logo.

Each card has my signature—yes, individually signed and not printed—inside. Very few people send cards these days so if you take the time to do so you are likely to stand out. The greeting card makes no mention about business; it's just a short message wishing the client the best this holiday season and my signature. The intention with a holiday card like this is not to push anything, as the card itself serves as a marketing piece because it keeps you top-of-mind with your client.

Living in Asia, I sometimes skip sending out cards during the Christmas holiday season and instead send out Chinese New Year greeting cards. That's me and my context; use your imagination to think of an appropriate moment in the year to stay top-of-mind and stand out from the competition with a personalized direct mail campaign.

In addition to the standard holiday greeting cards, I also have birthday cards, *Thinking of You* cards, and a card with an espresso machine and coffee cup on the front. The latter I use to either request a meeting or to say, "Thanks for the coffee," after a meeting has taken place.

All of these cards are branded with my company name on the back. I'm fortunate that the printer I work with doesn't set a minimum print quantity, so I can print as few or as many as I desire.

If you are concerned that minimums and cost might be an issue for you as a start-up, then skip the branded element for the moment and go out and purchase a handful of nice cards that you can use. The main point here is that it be a hand-written note. You'll be surprised how a small hand-written card can go a long way.

Now that I've taught you all I know about stationary, business cards, brochures, and greeting cards as a marketing tactic, allow me to introduce you to another one of my favorite offline tactics.

What I'm about to share with you might be one of those things that you say is not for you. Before you write this one off and move onto another section, hear me out. This could be a great addition to your marketing toolbox: article marketing.

Article Marketing

The offline tactic that I am going to introduce here can be translated online as well, but for our purposes here, I'll be discussing getting your articles published in your local newspaper, industry or trade publications, or magazines that reach your target audience.

To clarify, I am not talking about paying for a publication to appear in the paper, as in the case of an advertorial. With a little research, you will find which newspapers, trade publications, and magazines are open to receiving articles from industry experts like you.

When it comes to article marketing, you may be intimidated because you don't consider yourself to be a great writer. Get over it—you're not writing a novel! Writing an article for marketing purposes is, essentially, nothing more than sharing general information about your product or service and how it helps. A blog post is usually about 300 words. An article should be over 400 words, and a one- to one-and-a-half-page article would be about 650–800 words.

The simplest types of articles follow this basic format: an introduction, the body, and a conclusion. One of the easiest articles to write is a *how-to* piece, which starts with an introduction followed by the three to seven points (in sentence form) you wish to make and wrapped up with a conclusion. When deciding how many points to make, consider offering an odd number of points—three, five, or seven. For some reason people tend to gravitate to lists with an odd number of points.

That's not to say that you couldn't create an article of top ten widgets for social media, or eight gizmos to help you lose weight. There are no hard and fast rules that says you *must* use odd numbers; statistics just show that the conversion on these types of articles do better.[39]

Online Marketing (Digital Marketing) Tactics

You might be surprised that I have separated the offline from the online tactics. I wanted to make a point that it's not *all* about digital marketing. At the same time, it is true that more and more people spend time online—and yes, we need to meet the consumer where they are.

It's true that we live in a digital world, and that consumers often spend a significant percentage of their time online. However, if you focus only on digital touchpoints to reach prospects, you might find yourself swimming in a red ocean, competing for prospects' hearts and minds against everyone else in your industry or field.

To make the most of reaching your target audience, you will want to focus on multichannel marketing—that is, on- and offline channels.

Social Media Marketing

Social media marketing (SMM) is the process of promoting your site or business through social media channels and it is a powerful strategy that will get you attention, considerable traffic, and inbound links. (When other sites link to your site, this sends a signal to Google that your website has authority. Google's algorithms will take this into account and improve your listing position when people search for your particular product or service.)

SMM is a form of internet marketing that involves creating original and curated content and sharing that content on social media networks to achieve your marketing objectives. The process includes activities like posting text and image updates, videos, and other content that drives audience engagement.

If you're not speaking directly to your audience through any one of the many social platforms like Facebook, Twitter, Instagram, and Pinterest, you're missing out!

Notice I said, any one of the many . . . not all. It is not necessary for you to participate in every platform out there. Your goal will be to find the two or three that work best for your business.

There are no hard and fast rules as to how often or how much you should post. There are different schools of thought on this, and I believe it really comes down to a) what your objective is, b) what kind of content you are posting, and c) how much time you have to spend.

For entrepreneurs just starting out, you're doing great if you can post something two to four times a week and upload one blog post a week. (Stay tuned for a discussion about blogging.) Social media can be outsourced or you can manage it yourself; I'll discuss both of these options later on.

Three Important Aspects of Social Media

Social media allows a message to be replicated through user contact. Content becomes viral, and a buzz is created for your events, tweets, blog entries, and videos.

Find ways that the fans of your brand can promote you in multiple online social venues or communities using sites such as Twitter, Facebook, LinkedIn, YouTube, or Instagram.

Social media marketing is conversational. It invites people to participate, to interact with one another, to express their likes and dislikes—to have a voice. Social media marketing works best when it fully engages and respect users.

Your Website

There are some people who will tell you that you don't need a website for your business. I totally disagree. In this internet age, prospects are checking you out before they pick up the phone or contact you via email to request that face-to-face meeting. Without a website, it will be difficult or impossible for them to do their research about you in advance.

Many of the marketing tactics we use today are designed to create awareness and educate people about your brand and then send them to your website. Once they're on your site, you can capture their email details and then continue the conversation with them. The website itself is one of the ways this conversation takes place.

A website is a visual element that demonstrates who you are by setting a tone through design, colors, and fonts—in other words, it helps create the brand perception we've been talking about. While on your site, prospects can read more about you, what you stand for and how you help. On your client page they can learn who you help by reading testimonials. Videos and interesting articles will help build interest, rapport, and trust.

Your website can also offer more than one opportunity for prospects visiting your site to opt-in to your newsletter or download your freebies, also known as lead magnets. Since people will enter your website through different pages, it's a good idea to scatter these throughout your site.

Another reason a website is a good idea is that it's the home of your blog. Yup, your blog. That's the next online marketing tactic, and an important one that you'll want to consider as part of your marketing toolkit.

Blogging

Establishing a blog is another important online marketing tactic. If you were to select only two or three digital marketing tactics to use for your business, I would suggest that you seriously consider making blogging one of them.

A blog is original or curated content that educates and entertains your reader and ideally keeps them coming back to your website for more of the same. This content need not consist of long and arduous articles. A blog is a minimum of roughly 300–400 words and can be up to or over 1000 words. A blog allows you to express your personality and share your thoughts.

Blogging, should you decide to make this part of your marketing strategy, is one tactic that should be done on a regular basis. I would recommend once a week, or once a month at the very least. I get it that once a week might be a stretch when you're starting out; however it is something that you'll want to make a regular habit—not to mention it also helps with your website search optimization.

People often get stuck because they don't know what to write about. I've been there. Here's how you can get started with your first set of blog posts.

Make a list of the top pains and concerns that your ideal client or prospect is experiencing. List the top frequently asked questions your target audience might have for you. List the solutions you offer to address or resolve the prospect's pain points. Write out as many things as you can think of, and each of these issues can be a blog post.

Once you get good at blogging, you might get asked to guest-blog on other sites. This gives you a chance to reach new audiences. The most valuable aspect of guest blogging is the bio box that goes at the bottom of the post.

Your bio box gives your name, your company, two or three keywords built into the two or three sentence biographical write-up, and hyperlinks to your website, company blog, or maybe even a Facebook or sales page.

Email Marketing

If you were to ask me what are my top three must-have tactics for running a small business (or a large one), I would definitely say email marketing. It's simple to use, it gets you in direct communication with the consumer, and it can easily be set up to be automated.

In the upcoming chapter on using technology I've gone into great detail about how you can and should be using email in your business, so I won't discuss it any further here, but please do not skip that section—email marketing can do wonders for your business.

Now let's move onto another tactic that ranks high on my list of highly effective marketing tools and tactics, video marketing.

Video Marketing

You might be wondering why I've added video as a marketing technique, or you might be thinking it's not something that you want to even think about as a busy start-up entrepreneur. Read this, and don't gloss over it. Video marketing as a tactic can make a huge—and I do mean a huge—difference in your business.

Aside from the explosive growth in online video over the past few years, numerous studies show the following: users prefer video to text, users who watch video are more likely to convert into buyers, executives are more likely to navigate to a vendor's page after viewing video, and users who view videos are more likely to stick around on your site for longer. Think of it this way: if a picture is worth a thousand words, then a video must be worth a million. What better way for you to engage with prospects and customers than video?

According to video statistics compiled for 2017 by Blue Corona, almost 50% of internet users look for videos related to a product or service before visiting a bricks and mortar store.[40] Don't think for a moment that just because you are considering an online store that this doesn't concern you. Shoppers will be thoroughly checking out your online store too before they make a purchase from your site.

Why Video is Important for Small Businesses

It's clear that online video has become the form of digital media that consumers prefer. This does not mean that websites, blogs, or podcasts are dead. It does, however, mean that you need to rethink where you are focusing your online marketing budget. The truth is that video is not going away, period. This means that if you have a website and sell a product or service, you should seriously consider having a video presence.

In addition to the abundant statistics that show online video engagement is increasing, video has proven time and time again to increase conversions. (A conversion means that the user goes beyond simply viewing the website to purchasing a product, signing up for a newsletter, etc.)

Research shows that women decide to stay on a website or move on within five seconds, while men are a bit more generous with their time, staying at least ten seconds. A video on the home page and your other pages will keep people on your site longer.

While decent quality video production may have cost thousands of dollars in the past, expense is no longer an issue. With a variety of companies introducing stands and hand-held stabilizers for smartphones, virtually anyone with a smartphone can become a video producer—even you.

If you are thinking to yourself, "Well, the videos shot on those phones can't be very good," think again. Starting with the iPhone 4, Apple made a serious effort to improve the quality of the camera embedded in its phones, and with each new version they release the camera only gets better. The same goes for the Android phones; the Samsung Galaxy range of phones have some of the best cameras today.

This in no way implies that you must use a smartphone to shoot your video. But if money is an issue, do not exclude video from your marketing campaigns because you cannot afford expensive equipment. A fun video shot from a smartphone may come off as more authentic than a professionally produced video. That being said, be sure to keep it classy and professional. Just because you used the latest high-quality smartphone camera doesn't automatically mean it is a high-quality video.

By adding video to your site, you can keep prospects and customers focused and help them enjoy consuming your content. Video content is effective because it increases engagement with your audience in several ways. Videos are visually appealing and most of the people that you share your message with enjoy visual content.

Hosting videos on your website and YouTube also does wonders for your Search Engine Optimization (SEO). YouTube is the small business owner's best friend, and let me share why. In 2006 Google purchased YouTube for 1.65 billion dollars. This was well before the video-sharing site was anything like the platform it is today.

As Forrester Research reports, a video properly submitted (with title, tags, and description) is 50 times more likely to be ranked on the first page of organic Google search results (search results that appear based strictly on relevance, not the paid or sponsored results of a search) than other standard SEO techniques for driving traffic to your website or blog. "How is that?" you ask. Well, Google owns the YouTube brand and naturally Google prefers to promote its own brand first ahead of other web pages.

In addition, a thumbnail image of the video shows up in the organic search listings. Here's the exciting bit—a thumbnail image is 22 times more likely to be clicked on than the other listings, even if it is not ranked in the top three positions.

In addition to helping your website rank high in search results and increasing user hang time on your website, video provides a vehicle for educational content marketing. By creating valuable videos and sharing them on YouTube and your website, you cultivate trust with your audience and position yourself as an expert in your field. Think "digital infotainment."

As a business owner you have much to share. In fact, you have been speaking to your audience in some form or another since you started your business. The content that you are capable of sharing can be endless. Here are a few types of videos that will help you to get your message out in a big way.

Introductory Video

An introductory video gives you the opportunity to share high-value information about your product or service. Visually rich information is easy and fun to consume, so introduce your products and services in a way that appeals to your audience. Remember, though, attention spans are getting shorter. Sadly, it's now reported that the human attention span, at eight seconds, is less than that of a goldfish, which manages to pay attention for nine seconds.[41] Keep your introductory video snappy and to-the-point.

Tell Your Story

Think about what inspires you to offer your service or product to others. It doesn't matter what type of business you are in; you've got a backstory. When your audience understands what drives you to create content, products, and/or services for them, you build trust and credibility. When you share this information in a video you will increase your connection with the people that you want to serve. They get to see the essence of you.

Educate

You can enhance your expert status by being an educator in your field. Even though you are in business to generate revenue, you do not always have to promote yourself. Think of the topics that interest the people in your audience, and be the resource that provides valuable education on those subjects.

Even if you do not create the educational material yourself, the people who view you as a resource will appreciate your willingness to find and curate that material and to serve them with new and helpful information.

When prospective customers find you online, you can create a strong connection with the people that you want to serve. After all, you created your business to educate, to inspire, and to serve others. If you implement video into your business strategy, it will be easier and more enjoyable for people to find and consume the important content that you want to share.

Remember, this aspect of your marketing is not about selling, just entertaining, educating, and making a connection.

Putting It All Together—Creating a Marketing Strategy

Allow me to repeat what I said earlier about stringing marketing tactics together. The key is for you to look at the different tactics you decide to use and marry them together to create a cohesive strategy.

Creating a strategy doesn't have to be complicated. Remember, you're a start-up and so you want to develop a strategy that meets an objective within a predetermined budget over a predetermined timeframe. Yes, it's that simple.

Step one involves determining your marketing objective. This could be creating more awareness of your brand, generating more traffic to your website, gaining more readers on a blog post, getting more clicks on a Facebook ad, creating more leads, or converting more leads (in other words, making more sales) to name just a few.

Let's say you've identified generating more traffic to the site as your objective. Decide how many unique visitors you want per day and how long the campaign will run. The more specific and detailed you can be, the better, as this will give you something to measure your progress against.

Determine the budget. Knowing how much money you have allocated to the marketing campaign in advance will also determine the types of tactics you select.

Determine the campaign duration. I leave this as the last factor to decide on because in many cases the budget you set will ultimately determine how long you'll be able to run a campaign.

The platform you use for your campaign will depend on a variety of factors that we'll discuss next. Before you dive into your campaign you'll want to review the questions and instructions in the following Start-up Action Steps.

Start-up Action Steps

1. What kind of business you are in? Think about this in terms of the benefits to the consumer.

2. Set your sales and marketing goals and objectives.

3. Establish your monthly marketing budget, even if it's only $50–100/month.

4. Create the target audience avatar that you want to reach. An avatar is a character (man or woman) that represents the demographics and psychographics—and embodies the pain and desires—of your ideal client or target audience.

5. Decide what you want to accomplish with your advertising, publicity and promotion campaigns.

6. What is your timetable for achieving the marketing goals you outlined above?

7. Identify the marketing tactics best suited to your monthly budget and campaign objectives. Begin with the free items first and after that select tactics that are within your allocated budget.

Chapter 11

Suck It Up and Embrace Technology

Technology: I have a love-hate relationship with it. I love it when it works, and hate it when it doesn't. It frustrates me when I can't get something mechanical or technical to work. For many years the way I dealt with this was to go to my husband and tell him something on my computer wasn't working and ask him to fix it.

Often he would just go ahead and fix it himself; other times he would tell me what to do to resolve the issue. The problem with the latter was that I never paid attention to what I was doing, and didn't make mental—or actual—notes on how to correct the situation should it occur again.

Once when I was in Hawaii to meet with clients I was experiencing an issue I didn't know how to fix with my computer. I sat in my hotel room waiting for the clock to strike 6:00 am Singapore time so that I could call my husband to ask him what to do.

I guess you could say that I'm not by nature a fan of technology. I always felt that it just wasn't my thing. In fact, it was my husband who, in 1995, had to drag me kicking and screaming away from my beloved electric typewriter and fax machine and persuade me to use a computer and email.

Once I got into email and realized how much money I was saving by not sending international faxes, I was shamefully righteous in my attitude toward my clients, demanding that they start using email or I would stop doing business with them. Given my attitude you would have thought that I had been using email all along, and yet I had only been using email for about two months when I realized the significant benefits it offers.

Over time I learned to use the different applications that came with having the Window's Office program as well as other cloud based software programs.

My biggest learning experience with technology came about with the set-up of a new company website, which included an e-commerce platform as well. Once the website was up and running, I found it odd that the site would not come up in the search results when I typed specific key words into various search engines.

After a bit of investigation, I learned that my website creator knew how to make a pretty site, but knew nothing about the backend of the website. He had no key metadata on the home page other than the company name and our tag line.

At the time, I was selling children's golf apparel. The title page gave the company name, *kids-tee-off* and the tag line *quality can be fun*. In fact, he had the same metadata for *every* page of the site. With the way he set up the backend, how was Google or Yahoo to know that we were selling kids' golf clothes?

I had to take matters into my own hands to learn about the back-end of WordPress sites to get the website to rank on page 3 of search results. A bit more tinkering got me onto page 2, and eventually I learned how to tweak the site enough for us to finally rank on the first page.

Having gone through that arduous experience taught me a lot and I've learned how to quickly rank my other business sites, as well as clients' pages, on the first page of search results and in the top three to five positions.

If you had asked me ten or more years ago if I was technically inclined, I would have said no. There were so many things that I didn't know about a computer, and there are still to this day, but I can say I'm far more advanced now than I was back then.

The point I want to make here is that I didn't start out as someone with a technical bent. In fact, you might have said I was technophobic. It was out of necessity that I learned to embrace technology.

A few colleagues in my business circle are entrepreneurs in their 50s and 60s. We all had adopted a rather robust customer relations management (CRM) and marketing automation software program, and the learning curve was steep. I admit we all struggled to learn the system through our respective onboarding phone calls. Eventually we ended up teaching each other what we learned as we went along, yet we were only scratching the surface, utilizing just 10% of what the program could do.

Given the highly monthly cost of the CRM software, I felt that it was important to learn more of what it did by listening to the tutorials, playing around with the system, and tapping into the chat support. I felt great pride when I mastered some of the marketing automation features I'd been teaching myself.

When I shared my joy in having aced a new task with my other 50–60-something colleagues, they didn't seem to share my enthusiasm. Their response was, in general, that they couldn't be bothered to learn the technology; it was too hard and it wasn't something people our age could get a handle on. They would rather hire someone to do it for them.

Each time I heard this I wanted to grab that person by the shoulders and shake them. I wanted to scream, "Stop whining about how difficult technology is. Suck it up and get on board the train or you're going to get left behind!"

So, before you go there and begin complaining that you're a dinosaur and that you can't learn how to use software apps for your business, I'm here to say to you, "Suck it up! Change your mindset about the value of learning new, difficult things. You can do it!"

Will you be able to master different types of technology overnight? No. But you've got to start somewhere. You need to embrace technology for your business, and it's going to make your life so much easier. Trust me on this one.

Technology is Your Friend

As a new business owner you probably feel rather intimidated looking at the various software applications (apps) out there for you to use. If I were just getting started I would likely feel the same way.

Technology is going to make it easier for you to do more with the limited time, money, and manpower you'll have at your disposal. You will soon come to realize that technology truly is your new BFF, especially if you are a solopreneur.

The good news is that software suppliers are getting smarter when it comes to follow-up support. Many offer onboarding trainings that walk you through the elements of the program and show you how to use it. Many have tutorials that you can follow—and then of course there are always your two best friends, Mr. Google and Mr. YouTube.

You are perfectly within your rights to outsource someone to do some of your time-sensitive, technology-based operations such as auto-responder emails and marketing campaigns. Having said that, I believe that it's important for you to know how to use the program and then, once you know the basics, you can always hire a freelancer to do the actual tasks.

There are many done-for-you service providers out there waiting to assist you. But first you need to know the ins and outs of the software programs you choose to work with so that you can more efficiently instruct a freelancer on what you'd like done.

Let's take a look now at a few technology must-haves for business owners.

Set Up a Website

Some people in the business world will tell you that you don't need a website for your business, that you can forgo having one. Don't listen to these voices. Consumers today are better informed than ever before, and it's because they generally research products and services online before contacting a business. Your website gives consumers the opportunity to learn about your products and services and the solutions that you provide—specifically how you can help them. People will check out your website first and then determine whether it's worth their time to pick up the phone or send you an email.

Now let's talk about the steps you need to take to get yourself up and running and ready to be discovered online.

Register Your Domain Name

First things first. In the chapter about creating brand perception we discussed the importance of coming up with just the right name for your business. Once you've taken the time to do this, the next step is to obtain the business domain name. Grab it as soon as you can, as some domain name registries get sneaky and raise the price when you come back to secure the domain name later.

When you seek your domain name don't be surprised if it is unavailable. For many newbie entrepreneurs, securing a domain name for the business is a poorly timed afterthought.

Several years ago I mentored a few fashion design students. One day I was working with a sweet young lady on her brand, I asked her if she had secured her domain name. While we were working together I learned that she had not secured her domain name yet, so I immediately conducted a search for the name of her business to see if it was taken. It took a few moments for the page to load so we turned our attention back to what we were doing. When I looked up again, we were both shocked by what we saw. We had been connected to a pornography site. I'm sure that poor girl saw things on that page that she could have never imagined in her wildest dreams, and she went completely red in the face.

To make a long story short, the domain was already taken. In the end, we took the original name and dropped some of the vowels so that it read the same way without having to use the full word. And no—I'm not going to mention that word here. Sorry guys.

According to Key-System's European Domain Centre there are up to 882 domain extensions available in the world.[42] Ideally you will want to find a name with a *.com* ending. Consider registering variations on the name so that you can protect your name and, more importantly, protect yourself against other people trying to infringe on your brand or hijack your brand identity.

On a separate note, I would also suggest that you register your own name, even if you aren't planning on using your name for the business. This is one domain name that you certainly don't want other people to hijack.

And it might sound like a bad joke, but you should consider registering your name with the domain extension *.sucks*. Yes, you read that right. Myname.sucks. Let's face it, there are some disagreeable people in the world who, if they really want to make your life miserable, could easily register a domain name under your name with the *.sucks* ending. All they need to do next is host the site or blog, add some nasty comments about you, and *bang*, there it is in the search results. The best way to protect yourself from this happening is to buy the domain name so that no one else has access to it. Consider it one small step toward protecting your name and your reputation.

Another thing on domain names: don't get sucked into the scam of someone looking to sell you a domain name at a hefty price, and don't go to an auction to buy the name at an enormous cost either. As I already mentioned, there are so many different domain extensions available these days that you are sure to come up with something that works well for you.

Some of the sites that you can use to register your domain include Blue Host, 1&1, GoDaddy, Network Solutions, and iPage. I would suggest you check out all of them, as things change over time. Some of these companies offer hosting services as well.

Source a Hosting Company

Once you've secured your ideal domain name, the next step is to find a service provider to host your site. You can easily search for hosting companies and you'll see that some of the domain name providers discussed above also offer hosting services.

It's so important that you look for a reputable company to host your site. I know that you want to save money as a start-up, but this is one area where you do not want to be pinching pennies. Remember that you get what you pay for.

One of the things I suggest you do when buying software packages, including hosting, is to purchase for a year or two. With hosting and similar services billed annually, you don't have to worry about the month-to-month expense when cash flow is an issue at the outset of your business.

Create a reminder for yourself so that you don't forget to renew when the time comes to do so. You don't want your site to be down temporarily because you forgot to renew the hosting.

One very important detail to inquire about with your hosting provider is whether they keep back-up files of your website content and structure, in the event your site goes down or the site is hacked. Not everyone provides this service, or at least not for free, so find out before signing up.

Finally, look to see if you can also purchase a maintenance package for the website. It's really valuable to be able to call on someone to help you when you're still new to figuring out the backend dashboard or if you encounter something that requires technical expertise beyond your own.

Purchase a Website Template

Gone are the days when you had to hire someone to custom build your website. Today you can be up and running in a day if you tap into prefabricated websites that you just tweak and you're ready to rock and roll. Needless to say, you need to prepare your content in advance so that you can just cut and paste when you're ready to build your website.

One of the easiest ways to start, when it comes to designing your website, is to use a cloud-based website builder. E-commerce sites such as Wix, Weebly, and Shopify allow you to pull together a customized website within hours, using drop and drag functionality, and you don't need to have any technical expertise. These sites are applicable to a variety of industries.

Another fantastic way to get started with building your new website is to purchase a template from Joomla, Kajabi or WordPress. Website templates are a bit more robust and offer more customizable features than the DIY e-commerce sites listed above. It used to be that the free templates were pretty basic and—let me just say it—ugly. Today even free templates can be very useful and beautiful. The advantage of purchasing a website template is that there are hundreds of pre-made designs that you can customize. My experience has been with WordPress templates, so I'll use them as my focus in this discussion.

As I told you earlier, I didn't start out as a techie. Using the WordPress dashboard (the backend) is fairly easy once you get the hang of it. If I can do it, so can you. Remember, this section is all about embracing technology. Trust me, it is going to make your life so much easier once you learn how to automate various functions of your business.

There are so many websites offering templates that I won't try to list them here. I've selected a few WordPress template providers for you to consider, such as ThemeForrest.com, ElegantThemes.com, and TemplateMonster.com. When you've narrowed your search down to a few templates that you like, make sure you read the reviews and take note what the star rating is. The more stars the vendor has, the more likely you are to be satisfied with their template.

Now that you've registered your company domain name and found a template and a hosting company, you're ready to set up your website. The next thing you're going to need for your business is an email service provider.

Email Marketing—Utilizing an Email Service Provider

It's inevitable in this digital world that you will have a personal email account, perhaps two or three. It's become the main way we communicate with one another, even with our close friends and family. It's how we stay in touch. Think about it—when was the last time you picked up the phone to have a conversation with an old friend? Even now I rarely call my family on the phone—we Skype instead. Alternatively, we use email to stay in touch.

In this section I want to talk about the importance of staying in touch regularly with your clients and prospects. The easiest and most cost-effective way to do this is via email. This method of communicating with your community and prospects is referred to as email marketing.

This means you will need to embrace using technology—in this case, an email service provider—to make use of email marketing. Email marketing is one of the top "must do" strategies for marketing your business.

Chances are you have a personal email account using a service provider such as Gmail, Outlook, Hotmail or Yahoo. When you use Yahoo or Gmail as your service provider for your company and your email address looks something like mycompany@yahoo.com, it makes your business appear amateurish. It signals to the world that you don't take yourself seriously or make the effort to use your business domain name. It doesn't cost that much for you to purchase an email address under your domain name.

Once you've secured your email with your domain name, the next step is to sign up with an email service provider that allows you to capture your website visitors' email addresses via an opt-in form. This will allow you to include those visitors on your mailing list for pre-scheduled email campaigns, otherwise known as auto-responder messages.

There are different levels of service providers offering bulk email distribution and email campaigns for start-ups, enterprise businesses, and multinational companies. Some players that have been around for a while include MailChimp, Constant Contact, Aweber, Active Campaign, and more robust systems such as Infusionsoft. MailChimp is the easiest of these options to get started with, and is also the cheapest.

When it comes to marketing your business, one thing you should strive to do every day is to build your list of prospects so that you can build relationships with them and speak to them on a regular basis.

While most people who visit your website won't be ready to buy from you immediately, they may consider making a purchase later. You don't know where people are in their buying cycle, so regular contact with them keeps you top-of-mind with them.

When you stay in touch and educate prospects with news and information that solves their problems, answers their questions, or addresses their greatest challenges, you are building rapport. I refer to this strategy as keeping the conversation going.

And remember that people do business with people they know, like, and trust. The emails you send out are ultimately building trust with your ideal client. It's not enough just to set up an email marketing campaign; you need to ensure that you are giving your subscribers, the people in your tribe, value in each email or newsletter. That means providing them with content that is high quality, educational, and entertaining. Engage your readers by adding interesting images, static banners, audio clips, and video.

Email is particularly effective in maintaining existing relationships. Adding video to an email campaign markedly increases your message's power, influence and attraction. I'm all for adding anything that will increase my open rates, or the percentage of people who open the email. With engaging images, video, and a strong headline, the chances of your email being opened go up significantly. Consider these statistics:

> People spend on average 2.6 times more time on pages with video than on pages without.[43]

> Four times as many customers would rather watch a video about a product than read about it.[44]

> On Facebook, 85% of video is played without sound.[45]

When it comes to video, it might be something you record yourself to introduce you and your company, or it might be stock footage you compile to tell your story.

The images and stock video footage can be sourced from a variety of stock photography sites. Once you are ready to add images or stock footage (short video clips), look for royalty-free stock photography.

Royalty free is a type of license that gives you permission to use a stock image in certain ways without paying a royalty each time you use that image. Once you've purchased a photo, illustration, or vector image, you can use the image in several projects without having to purchase any additional licenses.

You can find quality royalty-free images for anywhere from 1 to 20 USD, though you could pay $100 or more with certain sources. For images that you'll use for your e-newsletter, blog, or on a Facebook post, you will probably manage to find satisfactory images for under $5 each. For digital purposes you don't need high resolution; an image that is 72dpi is usually sufficient.

The Importance of Building an Email List

As you dive deeper into entrepreneurship, you're likely to encounter the expression, "The money is in the list." To some, the idea of lists may bring to mind cold-calling and spam, but in fact there are different kinds of lists, some of which are incredibly valuable.

The lists that really count are lists that you build. They are comprised of people who have opted in to receive content from you. In other words, email lists are lists of people who have given you permission to market to them. Where else in the world can you get qualified leads (prospects) who explicitly give you permission to contact them with valuable information and occasionally make them an offer? Email lists are invaluable because they are made up of people almost waving a sign saying "Hey, share some great content with me or sell me something, please!"

There is no way for you to stay in contact with prospects unless you capture their names and email addresses—or at the very least, their email addresses.

Now let's move onto the next bit of technology that you'll want to consider for your business, a CRM system.

Utilize a CRM (Customer Relationship Management) System

Kudos to you if you're still with me after making it through the section on setting up a website. Hopefully you are absorbing this information in bite-size sections. The last thing I want is for you to feel overwhelmed by it all. Take a few deep breaths, grab your pen and paper, and let's keep going.

What is a CRM System?

I'm going to make this easy. If we were doing things "old school," we would keep all our client information in a Rolodex. (As a 50–60-something you'll know what that is so I don't have to explain!) Fast-forward 30 years and the business world now uses CRM systems. Needless to say, a CRM system is a lot more advanced than just keeping business cards in alphabetical order, and it serves multiple purposes.

Customer Relationship Management systems originated in the early 1970s. In simplest terms, a CRM system allows a business to manage client relationships together with the information and data that is associated with each client. Given that most of the systems are cloud-based, you can store prospects and client contact information as well as your accounts, your leads, and your sales opportunities in one central location.

Some of the features of a CRM system include:

➢ Store company names, contact person, email and telephone numbers

➢ Manage deals and sales within the pipeline

➢ Create, send, or trigger marketing campaigns

➢ Send emails from the system

➢ Store opportunities and quotes

➢ Track team tasks and events

➢ Design lead capture forms and landing pages

➢ Schedule meetings with clients

➢ Send client SMS

With all that information stored in the cloud, you can access it anytime, anywhere.

As a new business owner, you may be thinking that you don't need a CRM system because you are just starting out and you may not have any customers to put into the system. While that might be true for the moment, you will have prospective clients to target and this information can be stored within the CRM system, which will then grow with your business.

The CRM system is more than just a place for you to store clients contact information. It allows you to monitor the various stages of the sales process, otherwise referred to as the sales pipeline.

As you collect new leads through your various lead generation tactics, the names and email addresses of these new prospects can be added to your database as warm leads. Once they're in the database, you can put in place an automated email marketing sequence (also referred to as an email campaign) that allows you to communicate on autopilot with this prospective client.

Based on whether the prospect's response to these messages is positive or negative, the CRM system helps you to keep track of their interest, allowing you to identify warm prospects who are now becoming hot prospects in need of more active follow-up on your part.

Given the robust nature of CRM systems available today, just reading their *what we do* page can be overwhelming to the newbie entrepreneur. Bear in mind that you don't need to start with the top-of-the-line CRM. Key players in the market include SalesForce, Infusionsoft, and HubSpot, and a Google search will help you find many more.

Companies that allow you to use their entry-level CRM system for free include HubSpot, Zoho CRM, and Agile CRM. Pipeliner CRM allows you a two-week free trial period.

HubSpot (a Google-owned company) is by far the best free CRM system because there is no limit to the number of team members, or company users, you can add, and it remains free if you don't have more than a million contacts. I think it's safe to say that once you have over a million contacts in your database, you can afford to upgrade to the paid version.

Social Media Management Tools

Aaahh . . . here we are on the subject of social media. This is one of those topics where some time-management gurus will tell you to not even bother with social media, since it is a time-suck, and other marketing specialists will tell you that it is a must. Two sides of a coin—and I can see both points of view.

I think it really comes down to what your objective is for using social media. Social media or content marketing can be used for a variety of reasons depending on your desired outcome. It can be used for lead generation, distributing content—yours and other people's content—and to build a tribe or community or to create awareness.

I know plenty of people who don't bother with daily social media posts. They post only when they want to share something with their community. Once I heard a very well known person in the professional-speaker community ask the audience at the National Speaker's Association Conference, "Why would you do this if it doesn't bring you any business?" It made me pause for a moment to ask myself, "Yeah, Pam, why are you really doing this?"

Following that conference, I sat down and really asked myself why I post on social media and what I want to get out of it. Once I'd asked the question I was able to get clear on what I wanted, and then I developed a strategy to meet that objective.

When I decided that I would develop the 50–60 Something Start-up Entrepreneur movement, I knew that I would need to start building a tribe, a community of like-minded people who were either entrepreneurs or thinking about becoming entrepreneurs. Therefore the content, tips, tools, and techniques that I produce or share on social media are centered on entrepreneurism for the over-50 crowd.

I set up separate Facebook and Twitter pages where this community could share their thoughts and ideas around being part of the #Fifty60Revolution. These are places that I can be with my peeps.

After I had figured out my *why* for participating in social media, I was able to formulate a strategy.

Now, if I go back to the viewpoint that social media is a black hole in terms of taking up your time, there is a part of me that agrees with this on a personal level. I will admit I'm not on Facebook every day. It's not where I choose to spend my spare time, and I prefer to check it out either in the evening or over the weekend.

From a business perspective, I'm fully aware that it takes time to generate content for your tribe.

Earlier I talked about using a VA for content, and I would highly recommend that you hire someone to help with this once you are established and ready to do so. But I'm going to advocate that while you're starting out you hang onto your money for a while longer and generate your content yourself.

That being said, I don't want you to spend hours every day working on this, so I'm going to share with you a way to manage your social media postings by using a social media management tool.

What is a Social Media Management Tool?

When it comes to running your business, you can't afford to spend all your time crafting tweets and scheduling Facebook updates. A social media management tool saves you time by keeping all your accounts (Facebook, LinkedIn, Twitter, etc.) accessible from one dashboard.

The dashboard allows you to write content once and then post to multiple platforms and to schedule the time and date for the content to go out. There is no need to separately go to Twitter, LinkedIn, and Facebook to upload content on each of these sites. You can do it all in one place, and do it only once. This can be a huge time saver.

I've used a variety of social media management tools over the years; some through a free membership and some as paid subscriptions. You'll find that the free versions have limitations and that to do what you really need to do, the upgrade to a paid version is probably your best bet.

Some of the top social media management tools include Buffer App, TweetDeck, HooteSuite, Social Oomph, Co-Schedule and GrowSocial. In the past I have used Hootsuite and Buffer App, and my current favorite is Co-Schedule. One of the things I like about this platform is that there is no limit on how far out I can schedule my content. At one point in time I had my content scheduled five months out—something I was able to accomplish with the help of a student intern.

Like any software program or application, these programs, which are similar in what they do, all have their pros and cons. And given that these programs change so often, making detailed information on them obsolete, I've chosen not to write individual reviews of them here. If you're looking to keep things lean and mean for the moment, then search Google for *free social media management tools,* check out the top three to five, and make your decision.

Let me warn you right now, there are going to be some folks who say that posting content using a dashboard is "cheating" or "not authentic." They are entitled to their opinion, but in *my* opinion, that way of thinking is rubbish and doesn't apply to the everyday Joe or Jane striving to run his or her business singlehandedly. Your goal is to get content out to your tribe *and* focus on the other important things in your business—like making a sale.

Scheduling content in advance means that you can still have a presence on the web and connect with your community even if you are out of the office or on holiday. I'm a big advocate for pre-scheduled content.

During my mother's last months battling cancer, I could step away from my business weeks at a time to spend quality time with her. Given that the content had already been scheduled, most people never knew that I was gone and they continued to interact with me socially as if I was posting at that moment. Every other night I would pop online for a few moments to respond to any comments that were made on the posts.

Time is money so do consider using one of these tools. I recommend that you set aside 30 minutes to an hour each day to do your initial posts and build up a reserve or a few weeks' worth of posts. Thereafter, carve out time in your diary twice a week (I like Mondays and Thursdays) to spend 15 to 20 minutes to add a few more posts.

You'll find that this will get easier as you go along and you might even be able to drop this down to once a week.

If you're thinking about having a virtual assistant manage your social media posting (stay tuned for more on this later), I'd suggest that you use a platform that allows for multiple users. This way you maintain your own user name and password and you keep yourself as the primary admin person, should any issues arise and you want to terminate the working relationship. It's important to stay in charge of your own account.

This chapter on embracing technology has demonstrated that there are a few key elements that you'll need to put in place for your business. The Start-up Action Steps will to walk you through what you need to do to get going, so grab pen and paper and if you're ready, your credit card—go secure your domain name and hosting service.

Remember, technology is your new BFF.

Start-up Action Steps

1. Setting up your business website will involve the following:

    a. Secure your domain name.

    b. Find a web hosting company.

    c. Search for and purchase a responsive website template that suits your needs.

    d. Determine what you want to feature on your site, such as articles, products, resources, videos, about you, about your clients, etc.

2. As an alternative to the steps outlined above, set up a site on Wix.com.

3. Sign up for an email service provider. Look at MailChimp or Constant Contact, which are the least expensive options for starting out.

4. Consider a CRM provider combined with an email delivery system such as Agile CRM.

Note: Go ahead and start working on your website; it won't be visible to the public until you make it go live.

Chapter 12

You MUST Become a Salesperson

When I look back over all the chapters in this book, I find it interesting that the chapter on sales appears as one of the very last. I wonder if that's because sales was something that I avoided for such a long time and so I've left it for last even here?

Let me pause for a second so I can slap myself. I know better now and the last thing I want to do is to give you the impression that selling is not important, that it is something to be left for the last moment or done as an afterthought. Now you can slap me too, because sales *are* so important. They're the lifeblood of your business.

I can already hear you saying "That's not me. I don't want to have to become a salesman or saleswoman!" I know, I know, you would just rather deliver your product and service than to go out and sell your product, let alone yourself.

Listen, I hear you. I felt the same way in the early years of my business. However, I'd be doing you a total disservice if I didn't push you to get over your natural aversion to the idea of being a salesperson.

Selling is merely the conversation between a potential buyer, or prospect, and a salesperson with the aim of selling products and services to that prospect.

Most people don't like to do the selling portion of their business because there is a tendency to think of selling as a sleazy or heavy-handed thing to do. It's a shame this negative perception of the sales role is so engrained in our minds, for this mindset could really be the demise of a business, killing it before it's even gotten off the ground.

So, as your friendly advisor, I'm telling you right now: you MUST become a salesperson if you intend to bring in business.

I'm going to confess something that I wouldn't want most of my immediate colleagues to know. I take pride in myself for learning how to market my businesses over the past ten years. I have good brand awareness and name recognition within my region, and I am proud of how I have constructed various marketing tactics and drip campaigns. However, when I looked at what was happening within my training and development business at the seven-year mark, I wasn't doing as much business as I thought I should be doing.

To be honest with you, when it came to sales, I thought I didn't need to do any prospecting for my business. I was arrogant about my business situation, believing that I didn't need to do any selling because clients would find me through my website. I had enough business in my pipeline, so to speak, and so I didn't go out of my way to look for new business.

Suffice it to say, I was operating under the *Field of Dreams* sales model, the "if I build it, they will come" mentality. That stuff only happens in the movies.

I finally had the realization that I wasn't earning more or doing more business was because I wasn't making offers. In a nutshell, I wasn't asking for the sale. "Hello Pam, why didn't that occur to you earlier?" I was operating under the pretence that if I put my brand out there and my website was beautiful, the sales would automatically happen. That was just wishful thinking.

My second *aha* moment was the realization that my offer was limited to one product offering, which was in-house training. The in-house corporate trainings weren't something that was marketable to enough people, and I had to figure out other ways to deliver my expertise.

You'll recall that in the chapter about *place*, I asked you to look at the different ways you can distribute your product or service. Now that you've identified these channels, you need to promote them as separate offers.

As was I writing this section I realized that there was a third *aha* moment in all of this, and that it was probably the most compelling of all. If I didn't get off my butt and come up with a game plan to go out and sell my services, I wouldn't be able to take care of my family, I wouldn't be able to eat, to put a roof over my head, or to pay my bills. It was if someone had hit me in the head with a brick. It was a scary realization and I knew I was going to have to suck it up, get over my negative beliefs around selling, and get to it.

I was allowing my fear of asking for the sale to get in the way of my own livelihood. As a 50–60 Something Start-up Entrepreneur, you simply can't let this happen. There are far too many reasons that we as a demographic need to get this part right. The goal is not for you to just survive—we want you to thrive in your new venture.

Believe me, the desire and need to be a good at sales becomes really clear when the cash flow starts to get low. There is nothing more motivating than catching a glimpse of rock bottom in your business bank account.

If your financial situation is sound and have chosen to become an entrepreneur because it was your plan all along, then good for you. However, you're still going to need to sell, so keep reading.

I'll be the first person to admit that I'm a natural marketer. However, I still dug in and learned about the *process* of prospecting and selling. I just kept reminding myself that I had a great product to offer *and* I needed to take care of my family—"So just do it, Pam!"

Ok, roll up your sleeves and let's look at the very important topic of sales and the process of prospecting and creating your sales pipeline.

Start with a Positive Mindset

I'm all about mindset, so let's address mindset issues around selling. Quantum physics' Law of Attraction says that you get what you think about, so you might as well think about what you want. If you walk around thinking that selling your product or service is going to be difficult, then guess what? It will be difficult.

If, on the other hand, you think sales is something that you can pull off with some effort and a good, strong game plan, then you will see positive results.

Make the decision today: sales calls are just another part of your daily operations. Once I made the commitment to do this daily, and to start it first thing in the morning, I came to see that it really wasn't all that bad.

Make Time to Prospect

You may have heard the expression, "You've got to be in it to win it." Most people are referring to the lottery when they use this expression, but I feel the same thing could be said about sales prospecting. You've got to be in the game of prospecting to win at the game of sales.

Step one is to carve out blocks of time for prospecting, ideally every day. If you are serious about securing new business, you've got to allow time in your day to do so. I would say 20 to 30 minutes should give you plenty of time to reach out and connect with a few people.

Step two is to block this prospecting time into your diary. What gets put in the calendar gets done, and you don't set aside time in your calendar for prospecting, it won't happen. Scheduling dedicated blocks of time into your day will increase the probability that good intentions will be translated into action and habit.

The key is to contact a specific number of people every day. Some sales gurus will tell you to make a certain number of phone calls every day. Phone calls are good, but the phone is not the only way. To me, it's about reaching out and connecting with people via phone call, email,

LinkedIn, or a greeting card sent in the mail. What's essential is making and maintaining a connection with prospective and existing clients.

Prospecting for Business

Today, buyers can now find most of the information they need about a company's products or services before they ever engage a salesperson in conversation. The balance of power has shifted from the sales rep, who once controlled the sales process, to the buyer.

As a 50–60 Something Start-up Entrepreneur, your role now is not so much that of a salesperson but that of a trusted advisor.

Now that you're created your new product or service solution to meet the needs of your target audience, you need to get more specific about who you help. To whom do you want to become a trusted advisor?

Prospecting, the first step in the sales process, is where you identify potential customers or prospects. It is the process of systematically finding and collecting names, creating a database of prospects, or leads, and qualifying and organizing them.

Sales specialist Mark Hunter, CSP (aka "the Sales Hunter") and author of *High Profit Prospecting: Powerful Strategies to Find the Best Leads and Drive Breakthrough Sales Results*, gives us a great definition for prospecting.

> *Prospecting is about focusing your efforts toward the person(s) with the greatest potential to deliver not just a sale, but also at maximum price. The easiest guideline to follow is to remember buyers who buy based on tactical reasons tend to be economic buyers. Buyers who buy based on strategic needs are solution buyers. Solution buyers will always provide you with a better option to maximize price.* [46]

Cold prospects are consumers or organizations you've identified as well qualified but that have little or no awareness of your company.

They can be reached through advertising, public relations, cold calling, and networking.

Warm prospects are people who have shown some interest in your product or services, either by following your company on social media or by signing up to your email newsletter. A warm prospect might have been referred to you by a friend or previous client. They may also be consumers or organization representatives with whom you've previously spoken or met. You've captured their contact information, which makes them more valuable than cold leads.

Hot prospects are the ones you've successfully moved through the first two stages of your sales cycle. They are the best type of lead to have, as they are qualified individuals or companies that are close to the buying stage of the sales cycle.

Identifying Your Ideal Prospects

Now that we've identified what prospecting is, the next step is to find the right prospects to reach out to. Your goal is to identify the types of companies or individuals who might need your product or service and then move them through the sales process from being a cold prospect to a warm prospect to a hot prospect ready to buy.

This might sound obvious, but before you can categorize your prospects as cold, warm, or hot, you need to have some prospects to categorize. Identifying potential customers early in the sales process is key to keeping a company's sales pipeline full.

Prospecting is about finding people who can and will buy from you. As a newbie to business you might feel intimidated when you hear people discuss the subject of prospecting, but it doesn't have to be a daunting process. Keep in mind that your aim at this stage is to find the leads that you can best serve, engage and eventually convert into customers.

As a start-up entrepreneur you've got multiple balls in the air at one time, so I'm not going to spout off that you need to spend all your time prospecting. It is a key element to the success of your business; however, you've got other things to do as well.

I've looked at prospecting for new leads from the viewpoint of a new business owner. I'm keeping it simple so that you have a process to get started with, and then you can always scale up the number of prospecting calls you wish to make or outsource some of your lead-generation activities later down the road.

Qualifying Prospects

After you've researched and identified your ideal clients (these are the people who you identified early on whose pain, problem, need, or desire you will resolve with your product or service) you can start using different methods to reach out to them. These tactics can include cold-calling, email, trade shows, direct mail, webinars, product seminars, and advertisements for lead generation.

Your time is a precious commodity, so you want to determine rather quickly if you are speaking to a tire-kicker or a real buyer. When you're in a conversation with a company or individual, you'll want to quickly assess them by using the BANT lead-qualifying system.

BANT is an acronym devised originally as an IBM sales strategy to determine if a buyer met the following criteria. As you go about preparing your list of prospects, determine whether they meet the following requirements of a qualified lead:

Budget: Does the prospect have the financial means to buy your products?

Authority: Can the person I'm speaking with make the purchase decision or do they answer to someone else?

Need: Does the prospect truly have a need that my product or service will fill?

Timescale: Is there a specified time when they intend to make a purchase?

A variety of questions will help you determine if the prospect has set or prepared a budget that has already been approved by management. Keep the following questions at the forefront of your mind.

Is the person you are speaking with the person in charge or are they the pre-qualifier? Are they on a fishing expedition because the boss really doesn't know what he or she wants or needs? Does this person have the authority to say yes to the proposal?

It's likely that a company will have already identified a need for a product like yours. In your various probing questions, it will be up to you to find out why they need it and for you to articulate how well your product or service meets that need.

Lastly, once you've gathered all the other information, you'll want to determine how long the sales cycle will take. This is a key piece of the puzzle as companies are sometimes gathering information for a purchase that might happen in the next year. If that is the case, then mark this in your CRM system so that you will be reminded to follow up again when they are ready to buy.

Remember BANT, and at the same time be prepared with your own series of questions to ascertain whether a prospect is a good fit for you. The better prepared you are, the more information you can draw from the prospect. Here's what I'd have you do if you were in a workshop with me.

Grab a piece of paper. Write down the phrase *who questions* and then the numbers 1 to 10 down the left side of the paper. Do the same thing with *what questions, when questions, where questions, why questions,* and *how questions.*

Now write as many probing questions as you can under each section. Be careful with your *why questions* as the word *why* can sometimes put people on the defensive, making them feel as they are being attacked or judged for a decision they made about a past or current product or service.

Here are some examples of the kinds of questions you'll want to ask.

- *Who will make the final decision about the company you choose to work with?*
- *Who else should be in this meeting?*
- *Who else in the company might benefit from our services?*
- *What can you tell me about your current situation?*
- *What have you tried in the past and how did that work for you?*
- *What will happen with your business if you don't take any action?*
- *What potential roadblocks might prevent us from moving ahead with this project?*
- *When would be an ideal time to get started?*
- *When would you like to take delivery?*
- *When would you like to schedule the appointment to see a demonstration?*
- *Where are you experiencing your greatest challenges?*
- *Where do you want to be six months, one year and two years from now?*
- *Where are you in the process of making a decision?*
- *Why are you starting this project now?*
- *Why are you considering moving to a new supplier?*
- *Why did you choose us?*
- *How can I make your job easier?*
- *How will you measure success?*
- *How does this project rank in priority compared to others you are working on?*

Given that the sales qualifying process may be new to you, it's okay if you go in with a list of questions to ask in your meeting. Over time you'll come to know what key questions to ask based on the type of company you are meeting with.

Asking pre-qualifying questions might seems like something so basic, something everyone would do naturally, yet you'd be surprised how many entrepreneurs and even big business sales reps skip this important step.

Design Your Sales Pipeline Process

It goes without saying that not everyone you reach out to on your list of ideal prospects is going to buy from you right away. They may have a need for your product or service solution at some point in the future. That could be three, six or even twelve months down the road.

Because many prospects are busy and not immediately contactable, they may not be ready to buy from you just yet. Therefore it's important that you have a process for making the initial connection and then keep the conversation going so that your brand name stays top-of-mind—which means that when they are ready to buy, they think of you. If you fail to stay in contact with them then you are opening yourself up to having them be lured away by the competition.

A sales process is a systematic, repeatable series of steps that map out and track interaction with prospects, from the first point of engagement with your business through to a close.

Ask anyone in sales and you'll learn that every salesperson has a different sales process, their own sales pipeline process for taking a prospect from a warm lead to a hot lead to a sale and then to the *wow* follow-up.

The sales process is simply the way you will stay in touch with potential customer; the means in which you will follow up. It's up to you decide what that process will look like.

It doesn't matter who you model yourself after or whether you create your own process, (which you most likely will); the key is to create a process for making the initial connection, qualifying that lead, keeping them in the pipeline or removing them if they are not interested or not a good fit (translation, they like what you have, but can't afford it), and creating an actionable system for following up and closing the sale.

It's important to always keep at the back of your mind that people or companies buy when *they're* ready to buy, and not when *you're* ready to sell.

You might recall from the chapter on marketing that it can take multiple contacts with a prospect before they even reach out to contact you. Likewise, once you have made a connection with a prospect, you must make a concerted effort to stay in touch with them. There are no hard and fast rules as to what the sales follow up process looks like.

Although it may take some effort to reach prospects, it's vital that you make each connection count. The big questions are, what makes for a good sales process, how should you connect, and how often should you follow up with a cold prospect before deciding they are not worth pursuing any longer?

The last question is a tough one; how you reach out and how often really depends on the lead temperature—cold, warm, or hot.

Unless you've already got connections from a prior job, chances are that as a new business start-up you are mainly going to have cold leads. For the sake of getting you started, I want to offer you a simple sales process to consider. Over time you can tweak this and make it your own.

Design Your Sales Prospecting and Follow-Up

1. Begin by making a list of your top 50 ideal prospects. Remember, these are people who meet the BANT assessment and who can pay for your goods or service. They should also be the type of company or people that you would enjoy working for.

   Next segment this list of people and companies based on the different outcomes they desire. In other words, what are the various ways that you can deliver your product or services? Go back to the chapter on *place* for a refresher on the different ways to offer a product or service.

2. Enter your prospects' contact details into the CRM system you have set up. When you upload the contact person's full name, job title, company name, and address (which is optional, but it could come in handy if you are planning on posting direct mail pieces or proposals), you can use tags to categorize and organize individuals or groups of people within your database for easy identification later. When it comes to sending out targeted messages, you can find the people who you've put into a selected group and then send a message out to them. Some of the tags that I use, for example, are *prospect, client, JV partner, supplier, speaker,* and *referral.*

3. Select two to three people per day that you will call in the morning.

4. Select three people per day that you will connect with on LinkedIn, and send them a message.

5. Select three people per day to whom you will send an email. Following Mark Hunter's suggestion, keep your email to a prospect short and to the point, as if you were writing a tweet or texting them.

6. Schedule one or two meetings per week with prospects or with someone who can make a referral.

7. Make two follow-up phone calls per day.

8. Join one or two networking functions per week.

9. Join two to three business meet-up groups, associations, or chamber groups. Attend regularly.

It's important to note that when you do stay in touch with your prospects, what you say or send out to them must be of value—of value to them, that is, and not just about you. Also, change up the message each time you reach out to someone. You can keep track of this information in your CRM system.

How Often Should You Follow Up?

If you are unable to reach your prospect by phone, leave a voice mail message or leave a message with the gatekeeper (in this context, usually their secretary or personal assistant). Always get the gatekeeper's name, thank them for their assistance, and list their name in your CRM system under the prospect's details. The gatekeeper controls access to your prospect and is therefore a valuable ally.

If you are unsuccessful in reaching your prospect on the first attempt, then for your second attempt consider calling one week later and leaving a message on their voicemail or with their gatekeeper.

Should you fail to reach your prospect on the second attempt, then for your third attempt schedule a call for three weeks later and leave a message on their voicemail or with their gatekeeper.

Wait four days before making your fourth attempt, which will take the form of an email indicating why you are trying to reach them. If you are unable to reach your prospect on the fourth attempt, call them one month later and leave a message on their voicemail or with their gatekeeper. Are you still unable to reach them? Repeat this process or a variation of it till you reach them.

Make note in your CRM system which message you left each time so as to not repeat the same message on your second, third, and fourth attempts. 80% of sales are made after the fifth to twelfth contact, so it pays to persevere.

Results of a study conducted by the Massachusetts Institute of Technology indicate that the most successful time to reach an initial prospect is between 8:00 am and 9:00 am and then between 4:00 pm and 5:00 pm.[47]

Avoid being a pest. If you call too often (daily or every other day) you'll look desperate.

Selling is a Necessity

As you can see, there is much to think about and to put into place when it comes to selling your products and services. Selling has a bad rap, so it's no wonder people want to avoid doing this part of the business. But it's a vital element to any business, and it becomes easier and more natural with practice and proper systems.

I suggest that when you're ready to put together your sales process, come back and reread this chapter, then lay out your plan of action. Do this in conjunction with purchasing your CRM system as the two go hand in hand.

Although you don't have your CRM system in place just yet, don't let that stop you from getting started with the sales process, as any information you gather can always be stored in an excel spread sheet for the short term. Hop on over to the Start-up Action Steps and get a jump on creating your sales process.

Start-up Action Steps

1. Determine your 50 ideal dream clients (companies or individuals you would like to work with).

2. List your Dream 50 in your CRM system. Upload company and contact names, email address, telephone numbers, and business addresses.

3. Design your sales follow-up process.

4. Screen your prospects using the BANT qualifying questions.

5. Determine which prospects you need to call to make contact.

6. Decide which prospects you will call to set appointments.

7. Decide which contacts you need to speak with to close a sale.

8. Determine how you will wow your client after the sale as part of your follow-up. You might want to consider addressing a personalized, hand-written thank-you card or a small box of chocolates to the key decision-maker, or making a financial donation on behalf of the client to their designated charity of choice.

Chapter 13

Overcoming Overwhelm

Since you've made it this far, I'm going to take the time to congratulate you. Your commitment to taking this all in says that you're serious about creating and operating a profitable business.

We've covered a lot of information as we put the Entrepreneurship Path Framework in place, and by now you might be starting to fill a bit overwhelmed.

Starting a new business is exciting and daunting at the same time. As a 50–60 Something Start-up Entrepreneur you may sometimes find yourself feeling more daunted than excited. My hope for you is that you spend as much time as possible in the excitement stage, and in that spirit I'd like to offer you some solutions on what to do to overcome overwhelm.

There is a good chance that your business will be a solopreneur venture, which means the success of the business rests entirely on your shoulders. This kind of pressure doesn't make starting your new company any easier.

Having started four businesses, three which I owned and operated myself and a fourth which I founded with shareholders, I totally understand that sense of overwhelm—trust me. I'd be remiss if I didn't mention that even after 25 years as a business owner I still feel overwhelmed on occasion.

This is a normal part of the entrepreneur journey. I've got your back and I'm going to get you through this. Listed below are some ways to consider to keep your head above water and maintain your sanity and sense of wellbeing.

Admit How You are Feeling

I may have said this before, but it bears repeating for the sake of our discussion here. I like to think of myself as a strong person, the gal who can do it all and doesn't need any help. I've been operating in this manner for so long that it has become part of my nature, and sometimes it is not a good thing. The downside is that outwardly I look like I've got everything handled, and as a result business acquaintances around me don't think to ask if there is anything they can assist me with. No one offers because I appear to have it all together.

I suppose I've become good at pretending to be Wonder Woman when I'm not. When I finally gave up my superhero cape and admitted how I was feeling, I became humble enough to share with a few close business buddies that I, too, needed help. When I finally opened up in this way, I felt a sense of release and I no longer felt tied in knots wondering if I was doing things right. Once they knew I was looking for it, my fellow entrepreneurs were only too happy to give valuable emotional support and business advice.

Starting a business with the attitude that you can do it all will only get you in trouble later down the road. Don't make the mistake I did. There is no shame in asking for help. In fact, the smart businessperson will do it often.

Now that you're ready to ask for help, let's look at some of the tools and solutions out there that will make your life a whole lot easier.

This is where I will introduce you to a host of ways that you can outsource services and projects when you might require assistance. I guarantee that "outsourcing" will become one of your favorite words.

Say it with me now, "Outsourcing." There are also ways to reduce the feelings of pressure and isolation and to become part of a community of like-minded business owners.

Don't Go it Alone—Get Help Through Outsourcing

Hiring full- or part-time staff can put added pressure on a start-up business, given the financial expenditure for salary and benefits. The great news is that it is easy to run a business start-up without the expense of full-time or part-time staff. Don't you just love that?

Virtual Assistants

The concept of the virtual assistant (VA) has been around for some time now. A virtual assistant tends to be a self-employed person who works remotely to help a business owner or small company. Depending on your requirements, your VA may work five hours a week, maybe more.

These individuals are not on your payroll; instead they are paid as contractors based on the agreed-upon hourly or project rate. This means they are responsible for taking care of their taxes as an independent contractor.

There are a variety of virtual assistants with a variety of different skills. Theoretically, a VA can do anything support staff can. However, their duties are not just limited to clerical work.

Here are just a few things that a virtual assistant can do for you:

➢ Data entry of business cards into a CRM system

➢ Manage your social media accounts

➢ Upload your blogs and email newsletters

➢ Research

➢ Email management

- ➢ Bookkeeping
- ➢ Appointment setting
- ➢ Calendar and travel schedule management
- ➢ Website management (simple to complicated backend dash-board tasks)
- ➢ Any time-consuming or repetitive tasks

I could keep going with this list, but you get the idea. By hiring a VA, you have the benefit of giving out work when you need it done without the additional benefits cost and the concern of paying a regular 40-hours-a-week salaried employee.

Employ Freelance Help

Another source for non-salaried assistance is to use a project-based freelancer. You can find freelancers for hire on platforms such as Fiverr.com, Upwork.com, Konsus.com, Guru.com, and Freelancer.com. This is where most of my outsourced work is placed. Not everything that you require help with will be an administrative job. I have hired people from all around the world to do various projects. Bonus: it's a rewarding feeling knowing that you are also providing work for other entrepreneurs.

I love this approach because it allows me, at any moment, to tap into a large pool of individuals ready to accept a project. I used to work with a local graphic designer who worked full-time during the day and freelanced at night. That meant I was at the mercy of her availability and schedule. The lead-time for a project was significantly longer than that of a freelancer on one of the platforms I've mentioned, and the prices she charged weren't necessarily the lowest either.

Today, when I get an idea that I want to execute immediately, I head straight to one of my favorite sites to outsource for the talent I need. At any given time, I can be running two or three creative design projects, a video editing with voice over project, or working with someone who can support me with marketing automation drip campaigns. You'll soon discover that freelancers can really help you accelerate the amount of work you can get done.

How Do These Sites Work?

Depending on the freelance platform, I can list the price (or price range) I'm willing to pay and then wait for the freelancers to bid for my project. This is how Upwork operates (Upwork used to be known as Elance.com and rebranded after a merger with oDesk.com).

On other sites, the freelancer will list the type of jobs, or gigs, that he or she is offering, and their fee for each job. Fiverr, for example, gets its name from the fact that most of the gigsstart at 5 USD. There are freelancers that offer services starting at $10, $20 and $50 based on the type of service that they are offering.

If you're looking for a simple, quick Facebook or Twitter timeline cover, then the price of $5 is reasonable for the task requested.

That being said, *you get what you pay for* should be your mantra when selecting freelancers. I will often select a higher-priced freelancer when I believe that this is a person who values their services and is therefore asking to be paid accordingly. To me this is also an indication that they are more likely to provide a better result. The key is always to read the terms and conditions of what the freelancer is offering so there is no miscommunication.

Another thing to take note of is that English is not a first language for many of the freelancers on these sites, so I encourage you to be patient and to write your project brief as simply as possible without sounding condescending.

The last point that I would like to make is that the most popular and in-demand freelancers may have a virtual queue of people signed up to use their services. Again, take this as a sign that they are very good at what they do (which you'll be able to see in their portfolio window pane) and therefore may be worth the wait.

The categories and services that you can hire a freelancer for are quite varied. You name it and there is probably a freelancer out there that can take on your projects—for a price.

The following are general categories, within which you'll find specialized freelance skills to suit your needs:

> Website development

> Mobile app development

> Software development

> Sales and marketing

> Creative design (graphic design)

> IT and SEO

> Bookkeeping and accountancy

> Video and voice-over

> Copywriting, ghost-writing and editing

Visit the various sites I've listed and browse around to see what is available. You'll be amazed by what you can have done virtually—yet another reason today is the best time to be an entrepreneur.

Part-time Interns

Another source of assistance for your business can come from interns. These are usually high school, college, or university students looking to supplement their education with some type of on-the-job training to gain experience in their field of study.

Interns can also be hired to do simple admin tasks or answer phones, run errands, etc. Those with more experience can take on technical tasks such as email marketing campaigns or social media posting.

Depending on the program, some internships are paid and some are free. One Asian university (which I won't name here) requires its students to do an internship as part of their course of study. The sad part is that the local employers know this and the students are paid next to nothing—and I mean next to nothing. In some cases, these students are working 40 hours a week. This can't do much for an aspiring worker's moral, and in my opinion you couldn't possibly get quality work under such conditions either.

I personally believe that if you pay an intern well, then they will do a good job for you. They stay hungry and eager to learn more. They feel valued for the contribution that they are making to your company.

When it comes to hiring an intern, I suggest you look to students in their final year of high school and older, to be assured of a certain level of maturity. It's also easier to work with an intern when they have some prior knowledge of the type of work that you need them to do.

Remember, the goal is for them to help free up your time so that you can focus on the revenue-generating activities at the core of your business. If it is going to take you longer to show them how something is done than to do it yourself, you might want to forgo an intern and hire a VA instead.

Get Emotional Support

Becoming an entrepreneur is one of the most rewarding things I have ever done, including my experiences with businesses that failed—because I learned from them as well. With my first business, I was a solopreneur. My second business was a retail boutique and apparel brand. The third was also apparel related, this time with staff and shareholders. In my current role managing my two brands, Experiential and the 50–60 Something™ Start-up Entrepreneur, I am back to being a solopreneur, enjoying technical support from my husband and outsourcing certain tasks to freelancers.

Let me say this to you now so you are prepared. The life of an entrepreneur, especially that of a solopreneur, can be a very lonely situation. Yes, you interact with people during the day, be it in person or online, but that's more on the surface.

Being solely responsible for the decisions and outcome of your business can be daunting, particularly when there is no one in your daily work routine with whom you can bounce around your thoughts and ideas.

Don't get me wrong. My intention is not to shut you down or put a damper on your dreams—not at all. My intention is to make you aware of how you might feel later, down the road, once all the hype and excitement of a new business starts to wind down and you're left with getting on with things.

So, before you reach the point of feeling isolated within your own four walls and in your mind, there are a few ways to overcome this type of lone-wolf overwhelm.

Attend Networking Events

It is so easy to be so focused on working on and in the business for ten hours a day that you forget to get outside of yourself and outside the office. Often, the isolation that we feel is self-imposed. We feel that we should be putting all our efforts into marketing and sales and we forget that there is life outside these four walls.

The best way to combat loneliness is to get out and meet other people. Attend networking events in your community and neighboring communities as well. This means you get a chance to meet new people, as opposed to seeing the same faces at the same events each time.

Check out your local Chamber of Commerce for upcoming events and look to see what Meet-Up groups might be of interest.

Don't just go to events to get out of the house, attend with a sense of purpose. Build relationships and discover whom you can help and who can help you. Make a point to connect with at least three people and then be sure to follow up. The follow-up is where most people fail with networking.

If you're unsure of the ins and outs of how to become a great networker, then check out the book by the "Relationship Guy" Lindsay Adams, *The DNA of Business Relationships: How to Engage, Expand and Energize Relationships*. I've learned quite a lot from his book and by watching him using these techniques in person.

Mastermind Groups

It is by choice that I run my business as a solopreneur and that I outsource what I need help with. Outsourcing can support the side of your business where you need external services or projects done; however outsourcing doesn't support the need for business connections and emotional support. This is where mastermind groups come into play.

A mastermind group is a group of individuals who meet weekly, bi-weekly, or once a month, either in person or online. Mastermind groups offer a combination of brainstorming, support, shared connections, and resources together with peer accountability. The group objective is to tackle challenges and problems, provide support, and offer suggestions to those challenges. It is very much like peer-to-peer mentoring.

During the first meeting, you establish your own big goal and then map out a plan to achieve it. The group helps you with creative ideas for achieving your goal, challenges you, and holds you accountable. Mastermind members act as the catalyst for personal and business growth.

A mastermind group requires a long-term commitment so it's important that you find the ideal people to partner with. The group decides how often to meet and determines the agenda and the length of each meeting.

I've participated in a number of mastermind groups, some which worked well, while others did not. Based on my experience of what works and what doesn't, here are some suggestions to keep in mind should you decide to start a group or become part of one.

> ➢ Keep the group small, no more than six people. This allows you to get around to everyone in the group during your session.

- Have a mix of men and women. It's important to have different points of view.

- Fix the start time for 7:00 am. People willing to make a morning meeting demonstrate their commitment.

- Set the duration of the meeting to one and a half to two hours. If members want to stay on longer after the meeting officially ends, they can do so.

- Meet every two weeks on the same day and place. (This works well if everyone is in the same community. Otherwise alternate the location to accommodate everyone, but keep the same venues each time for the sake of consistency.)

- Set the agenda via email in advance of the meeting.

- Give each person five minutes to share his or her wins. Then begin discussing the topics outlined in the agenda.

- If only two or three people will be attending, the meeting still takes place.

In my mastermind experience, the group that worked best together was the group that met early in the morning. We chose to meet on Mondays because it was a great way to kick-start the week, feeling motivated and ready to achieve our big goals. That group stayed together for about two and a half years.

Look around your circle of entrepreneurs. Are there three or four people that have similar goals as you that will support you and become accountability peers for you?

Coaches and Mentors

Whether it's a life coach, a business coach, or a mentor, having somebody with years of diverse experience and perspective can help you broaden your own awareness about yourself, your business, and the competitive landscape.

A business coach or mentor can look at what you're doing objectively and assess your strengths and weaknesses while helping identify and direct your focus onto things that need work in your business.

A coach can help keep you accountable, and being accountable to someone outside the company can push you to a higher standard. Having a business coach also helps with that lone-wolf feeling we discussed earlier. It gives you the opportunity to have someone to bounce ideas off and to ask questions, and it helps to keep you motivated.

Keep in mind that nobody learns in a vacuum.

Support Buddies

Being part of a mastermind or having a coach offer great value. For me, the most enjoyable form of guidance, and probably the most beneficial in terms of accelerating my business, is a support buddy.

Chances are your support buddy will be another solopreneur. He or she may or may not be in a similar industry; what's important is that you share similar aspirations in terms of wanting to take your businesses to the next level. You might even share similar financial goals and big picture-dreams for your businesses.

A support buddy gets you—because you get him or her. When you share your grand ideas and plans for your business, your buddy will nod in agreement and support. Rather than smirking or ridiculing you for dreaming big or thinking outside the box, they will kick that box to the curb with you.

In many ways the support-buddy system is like a two-person mastermind group, but with more constant contact. You check in with this person often via email, personal calls, and text messages. It's possible to have more than one support buddy, as different people bring different things to the table.

Overall, a good support buddy pushes you to achieve your goals because they too are striving to achieve theirs and they want someone alongside them when they cross the finish line on those monstrous goals.

Because you are so like-minded and equally driven, you tend to achieve more in a short period of time. I've experienced this on several occasions when I take what has now been dubbed the "Power Business Retreat" with one of my support buddies.

The Power Business Retreat with a support buddy involves getting out of our home town for three to five days to a location with an idyllic setting that allows us to feel relaxed, yet provides an atmosphere for us to put our heads down and get some serious work done.

One of my ideal locations is a small, rustic beach retreat on a neighboring island with turquoise water to gaze upon and to swim in as well. I would rate it as a three-star resort with decent food, great staff who look after us, and clean rooms with the basic amenities.

The day starts at 6:00 am with a walk on the beach. We discuss our big dreams and outline the three to five things we aim to work on that day. Breakfast is at 7:00 am and by 7:30 we have started on the first agenda item. Once a project is complete, we move to the next one.

A short break consists of bobbing in the sea for thirty minutes while still brainstorming and discussing work. After drying off we move to a new location, start on a new project or topic, and eat lunch, which is followed by more work. By 4:00 it's personal time (massages or a nap) and we resume working at 6:00 pm. Dinner is at 7:30, with more discussion, and we're in bed by 9:30 or 10:00 pm—although on one recent trip, my buddy was so fired up to mind-map out his brand blueprint that he didn't retire until past midnight.

A retreat like this leaves you energized and motivated, with a major sense of accomplishment. I highly recommend you create your own Power Business Retreat twice a year.

As solopreneurs we all strive for success in our businesses. Don't fall victim to the downside of going it alone. Find people who can take on tasks and find the individuals who can provide you with emotional support as you make your way along the entrepreneurship path.

Attend networking meetings and partake in local Meet-Ups. Form a mastermind and find your ideal support buddy—or, if you're like me, several support buddies for diversity of input and support.

There are many people out there just like you who are part of the 50–60 Something Start-up Entrepreneur community and who are looking for mutual support. You just need to proudly raise your hand and say, "I'm part of the 50–60 Entrepreneur Revolution and I'm looking for a support buddy."

In the meantime, these Start-up Action Steps will help you create your plan of action for networking activities and for finding others who will support your journey.

Start-up Action Steps

1. Join your local Chamber of Commerce and start attending business events to network with other small business owners and potential clients.

2. Find a support buddy.

3. Consider hiring a mentor.

4. Outsource small, time-consuming tasks to a virtual assistant.

5. Spend an hour or two a week learning new technology or software applications.

6. Get out the office for a change of scenery.

7. Take a deep breath. Take another one.

Conclusion

ongratulations on the success of your new business. I know you may not have set it up as of this moment, yet the fact that you've come this far and that you've reached the conclusion of this book, says a lot. I believe that you *will* become an entrepreneur.

You came here seeking answers and solutions and I hope that I have provided you with enough information to get your business up and running.

The reality is that people in their 50s and 60s who lose their jobs will find themselves in an unexpected and challenging financial position.

At the time when we entered the workplace in the late 70s and 80s, we still believed that our lives would be like what we saw on TV—you know, the narrative where Dad went to work every day and kept the same job for ever. As kids in the 60s we witnessed women becoming independent, entering the workforce, and looking forward to a long-term career that they could be proud of. In essence, we drank the Kool-Aid and believed every bit of that lifestyle dream.

Fast-forward to where we are today, and that dream of a one-job career no long exists, whether you're a man or woman. That's not really going to cramp our style, since it's perfectly acceptable to have more than one job over the span of a lifetime.

What we didn't see coming, as 50–60-something men and women, is that we would fall victim to corporations worldwide looking to reduce their financial overheads by making us redundant. To survive the economic fallout of all this, we will push back to take control of our lives and our financial security by becoming entrepreneurs.

I sincerely hope that this book will be of significant help to you on that journey. Join the 50–60 Something Start-up Entrepreneur social media community, where you'll have the chance to interact with other men and women forging their own way. Here you will gain moral support as well as find a place to ask questions through the private Facebook group.

If you'd like to give yourself a head start with even more comprehensive support and strategies, consider investing in the 60-day 50–60 Something™ Start-up Entrepreneur online course.

You're going to be an awesome business owner.

Here's to your business success!

References

1. Mark Miller, "Older American Workers Struggle to Find Jobs After Economic Recovery," *Fortune*, September 8, 2016, http://fortune.com/2016/09/08/older-workers-jobs.

2. Ibid.

3. UK Office for National Statistics, *National Population Projections for the UK*, 2014-based, 2015.

4. Olivia Perkins, "Older Workers Suffer From Long-term Unemployment More Than Any Age Group," *The Plain Dealer*, March 23, 2013, accessed at http://www.cleveland.com/business/index.ssf/2013/03/older_workers_suffer_from_long.html.

5. TNS, February 2015, *Tracker Survey for Age UK (adults aged 50+ in Great Britain)*.

6. Department of Work and Pensions (DPW), *Fuller Working Lives: A Framework for Action*, June 2014.

7. Sarah A. Donovan, David H. Bradley, and Jon O. Shimabukuro, *What Des the Gig Economy Mean for Workers?*, Congressional Research Service, February 5, 2016, accessed at https://fas.org/sgp/crs/misc/R44365.pdf.

8. Ibid.

9. EY, *Is the Gig Economy a Fleeting Fad or an Enduring Legacy?*, 2016, accessed at https://gigeconomy.ey.com/Documents/Gig%20Economy%20Report.pdf.

10. Ian Brinkly, *In Search of the Gig Economy*, The Work Foundation (Lancaster University, UK), August 2016.

11. EY, *Is the Gig Economy a Fleeting Fad or an Enduring Legacy?*

12. Brinkly, *In Search of the Gig Economy.*

13. Pew Research Center, tabulations of March 2012 Current Population Survey, Integrated Public Use Microdata Series, University of Minnesota.

14. BrightStar Care, "Spread Thin: Caregiving and the Sandwich Generation," 2015, https://www.brightstarcare.com/resources/health-wellness/thin-caregiving-and-sandwich-generation.

15. Kim Parker, *The Sandwich Generation: Rising Financial Burdens of Middle-Aged Americans,* Pew Research Center Social and Demographic Trends Project, 2013.

16. Ibid.

17. OECD, *Society at a Glance—OECD Social Indicators,* 2011, *http://www.oecd.org/social/soc/societyataglance2011.htm.*

18. Oxford Economics, *The Longevity Economy,* September 2016.

19. Simon Kelly, "Forecasting Wealth in an Ageing Australia: An Approach Using Dynamic Microsimulation," (presented at the 7th Nordic Seminar on Microsimulation Models, Helsinki, Finland, June 13, 2003), http://www.natsem.com.au/storage/cp2003_005.pdf.

20. Heather Booth and Leonie Tickle, "Beyond Three Score Years and Ten: Prospects for Longevity in Australia," *Working Papers in Demography* 92, February 2004.

21. Government Office for Science, *Future of an Ageing Population,* 2016.

22. Oxford Economics, *The Longevity Economy.*

23. Ibid.

24. Todd Campbell, "The Shockingly Small Amount Americans Have in Retirement Savings," *The Motley Fool,* April 30, 2017, https://www.fool.com/retirement/2017/04/30/the-shockingly-small-amount-that-americans-have-in.aspx.

25. The United States Social Security Administration (website), https://www.ssa.gov.

26. Sean Williams, "A Big Social Security Change Is Coming in 2020, and You Probably Aren't Aware of It," *The Motley Fool,* May 27, 2017, https://www.fool.com/retirement/2017/05/22/a-big-social-security-change-is-coming-in-2020-and.aspx.

27. Jim Borland, "2017 Brings New Changes to Full Retirement Age," *Social Security Matters*, January 6, 2017, https://blog.ssa.gov/2017-brings-new-changes-to-full-retirement-age.

28. Skipton Building Society, "Do You Feel Prepared For Your Retirement?" December 7, 2016, https://www.skiptonfa.co.uk/knowledge-centre/do-you-feel-prepared-about-your-retirement.

29. Sarah O'Grady, "Savings Crisis: Millions Trapped as Retirement Will Be Delayed for Two-thirds of Workers," Express.co.uk, April 13, 2016, https://www.express.co.uk/finance/retirement/660440/Pensions-crisis-brits-work-into-retirement-record-low-interest-rates.

30. Age UK, "Later Life in the United Kingdom," August 2017, https://www.ageuk.org.uk/Documents/EN-GB/Factsheets/Later_Life_UK_factsheet.pdf?dtrk=true.

31. Medianet, "Are Australians Really Prepared for Retirement?" February 26, 2017, https://www.medianet.com.au/releases/126627.

32. Commonwealth Bank of Australia, "One in Two Australian Households Expected to Be Retire Ready," February 6, 2017, https://www.commbank.com.au/guidance/newsroom/commbank-retire-ready-index-2017-201702.html.

33. Small Business Trends, "Introduction to Franchising," December 2011, https://smallbiztrends.com/2011/12/introduction-to-franchising.

34. Jack Trout and Al Ries, *Positioning, The Battle for Your Mind* (New York: McGraw Hill Education, 2001), 71.

35. Satyendra Singh, "Impact of Color on Marketing," *Management Decision* 44, no. 6 (2006): 783–789, https://doi.org/10.1108/00251740610673332.

36. Nyla Smith, "Font vs. Typeface—What's the Difference?" *N-Vision Designs*, August 12, 2014, http://nvision-that.com/design-from-all-angles/font-vs-typeface-whats-the-difference.

37. Trout and Ries, *Positioning*, 32.

38. Alan Weiss, *The Consulting Bible: Everything You Need to Create and Expand a Seven-Figure Consulting Practice*, (Hoboken, NJ: John Wiley & Sons, 2011), 37.

39. Neil Patel, "Love 'Em or Hate 'Em: 9 Interesting Facts about List Posts," *Hubspot*, October 2, 2015, https://blog.hubspot.com/marketing/list-posts-facts.

40. Betsy McLeod, "50+ Must-See Video Marketing Statistics for 2017," Blue Corona (website), April 28, 2017, https://www.bluecorona.com/blog/video-marketing-statistics-must-see.

41. Kevin McSpadden, "You Now Have a Shorter Attention Span Than a Goldfish," *TIME Health*, May 14, 2015, http://time.com/3858309/attention-spans-goldfish.

42. European Domain Centre (acquired by Key-Systems in 2017), https://www.key-systems.net/en/blog/list-of-domain-extensions.

43. Ezra Fisherman, "Our Videos Dramatically Increased Our Visitors' Time on Page," *Wistia Strategy*, December 15, 2016, https://wistia.com/blog/video-time-on-page.

44. Megan O'Neill, "The Video Marketing Cheat Sheet," *Animoto Blog*, May 7, 2015, https://animoto.com/blog/business/video-marketing-cheat-sheet-infographic.

45. Sahil Patel, "85 Percent of Facebook Video is Watched Without Sound," Digiday UK, May 17, 2016, https://digiday.com/media/silent-world-facebook-video.

46. Mark Hunter, *High Profit Prospecting: Powerful Strategies to Find the Best Leads and Drive Breakthrough Sales Results* (New York: Amacom, 2016), 55.

47. Dave Elkington and James Oldroyd, "How Much Time Do You Have Before Web-generated Leads Go Cold?" (presented at MarketingSherpa's Business-to-Business Demand Generation 4th Annual Summit 2007, October 16, 2007), https://content.marketingsherpa.com/heap/DG07SFSlides/LeadResponseManagementReport.pdf.

Acknowledgements

The concept behind *The 50–60 Something Start-up Entrepreneur: How to Quickly Start and Run a Successful Small Business* and the desire to write it have been brewing in my mind for at least two and a half years. During that time, I witnessed how the changes in the economy began to really affect people in their 50s and 60s. When an immediate family member became the victim of corporate downsizing, I knew it was time to get moving and get this book out to the world.

It is one thing to have a book in your head, but it's another thing entirely to get it down on paper. Therefore, I want to acknowledge the people who helped to make this book a reality.

Many thanks to my "girl power" mastermind buddy, Lindley Craig, who totally gets me and supports me in achieving my big goals.

To "the Lindsay Adams," my book buddy and friend on this project. Thank you for pushing me and keeping me on track, and more importantly for helping me to dream and see the big picture and the long-term game.

To Darren Hardy, my online and High Performance Forum business mentor, who delivered on his promise of teaching me how to be better at marketing and sales and for helping me to identify the type of businesswoman I am—a White Knight and a Guru. I love taking on these roles.

To my younger sister Michelle Kennedy, who is always there to listen and to help me out, whatever the request may be.

And to Louisa Bennion, my editor and secret weapon. I am incredibly grateful for your professionalism, meticulousness, patience, and passion. You took my manuscript and turned it into a book that I am very proud to share with the world. It has been a pleasure to work with you and learn from you. Thank you.

Lastly, to my wonderful husband, John Wigglesworth. You stood quietly on the sidelines while I rambled on about this book and then you stepped up to lend support at just the right time. I love you very much. Thank you for your patience, and I am so looking forward to the journey this book will take us on.

Viva the 50—60 Something Start-up Entrepreneur Revolution!

Join the 50–60 Something Entrepreneur Movement

As a 50–60 Something™ Entrepreneur, you are now part of a very important movement—the movement that says, "Watch out world, here we come! We're not about to be pushed around by the corporate world. We are the new 50–60 Something™ Start-up Economy."

I invite you to join our community of like-minded start-up business owners looking to make a difference in their communities, for themselves, and for their families. Seek support from your fellow entrepreneurs by following me and participating with us on various social media platforms.

amazon Follow me on Amazon

Connect with me on Amazon and learn when my next book will be launched. You're in the 50–60 Something™ Start-up trenches, so I would love to get your thoughts as I develop the next book in this series. Help other readers know how the ideas you've encountered here will be of benefit to them by leaving a review of this book.

 ## Join the private Facebook group

Facebook.com/The 50-60 Something Start-up Entrepreneur

Connect with me and other business owners. Join the conversation or start your own. Share and learn from others in our private Facebook group, The 50–60 Something™ Entrepreneur.

 ## Connect with me on LinkedIn

http://sg.linkedin.com/in/pamelawigglesworth

You can find my articles on entrepreneurship, marketing and personal development.

 ## Connect with me on Twitter

Twitter @ExpPam

Looking for bite-sized insights on being an entrepreneur? Connect with me on Twitter.

 ## Subscribe and follow me on YouTube

www.Youtube.com/ExperientialSG

 ## Connect with me through email

Get in touch with me directly via email at pam@experiential.sg

Looking to take your learning to the next level?

It's great that you've picked up this book to kick-start your knowledge on how to start and run a business. Too often, though, we read a book and then fail to implement what we've learned. Sometimes you need more assistance to get things going, and then some support along the way. I'm here to support you in a variety of ways.

Hire me for your next event

You can hire me to speak at your next event. Contact me at speaker@experiential.sg for keynote addresses, one- to two-day seminars, corporate events, and business development retreats.

Accelerate your business start-up:

Tapping into my 25 years of experience as an entrepreneur and marketing consultant, I designed this online course to provide aspiring entrepreneurs with the sequential steps to set up and run a small business. This course will guide you through the creation of your product or service, (essentially your new brand), how to prepare your marketing strategy, and how to establish your sales distribution and overcome the overwhelm that can occur when you are a new business owner.

> Enter the discount code SSE150 at checkout and save $150 off the course registration fee.

The One-to-One Entrepreneur Accelerator Mentorship Program

Are you looking for personal guidance to accelerate your business start-up? Register for the 50–60 Something™ Start-up Entrepreneur online course together with the One-to-One Entrepreneur Accelerator Mentorship Program to fast-track your results. Get the help you need to kick-start your business as well as support and guidance over a period of six months.

> Enter the discount code SSE550 at checkout and save $550 off the course registration fee and the mentorship program registration fee.

About the Author

Pamela Wigglesworth, CSP, is an international **marketing** and **entrepreneurship consultant, speaker,** and the **managing director** of Experiential Hands-on Learning.

An American who has lived in Asia for over 27 years, she works with companies across multiple industries to increase their awareness, increase leads, and ultimately, increase sales. Pamela helps companies to strategize, systemize and monetize their business. In addition, she works with clients with to achieve high performance presentation mastery.

She is the creator of the SME 101 Marketing Bootcamp and is credited with starting the 50–60 Something™ Entrepreneur Movement and the 50–60 Something™ Start-up Entrepreneur online course in support of mature entrepreneurs.

Pamela has a WSQ Advanced Certification in Training and Assessment (ACTA) and has spoken or conducted seminars in Singapore, Malaysia, Indonesia, Brunei, Cambodia, China, Thailand, the Philippines, Vietnam, and the United States.

Organizations like Roche, Thomson Reuters, Starwood Group Hotels, MDS Pacific, Attorney-General's Chambers of Singapore, HSBC,

Brunei Economic Development Board, Malaysia's Media Prima, Olympus, TPG Capital, Singapore Press Holdings, the National University of Singapore, and more have hired Pamela to assist them with performance communication skills and marketing communication.

In addition to this book she is the author of *Public Relations* and *Small Business Acceleration: Get Noticed Using Facebook, LinkedIn, Email Marketing, Public Relations and Video Marketing*.

Pamela was a motivational speaker at the UN Humanitarian Affairs University Scholars Leadership Symposium 2013 in Manila, Philippines and again in 2014 in Phnom Penh, Cambodia. Invited by the United States Embassy Brunei Darussalam in conjunction with the Brunei Economic Development Board, Pamela conducted a series of workshops and talks on branding and marketing.

She is a member of the Global Speakers Federation and served as a past Vice-President of the Asia Professional Speakers Singapore (APSS). Pamela is a founding board member of the PrimeTime Business and Professional Women's Association in Singapore.

To learn more and about Pamela Wigglesworth, visit **www.experiential.sg**. You can also reach her by email at **pam@experiential.sg**

www.ingramcontent.com/pod-product-compliance
Lightning Source LLC
Chambersburg PA
CBHW070516160726
48003CB00004B/1584